The Motorless Flight Series

HALF MILE UP WITHOUT AN ENGINE:
The Essentials, the Excitement of Sailplanes and Soaring

THE GREAT AMERICAN BALLOON BOOK:
An Introduction to Hot Air Ballooning

MANBIRDS: Hang Gliders & Hang Gliding

THE WILD, WONDERFUL WORLD
OF PARACHUTES AND PARACHUTING

Books by Robert Gannon

Why Your House May Endanger
Your Health (with Alfred Zamm, M.D.)

Pennsylvania Burning

Great Survival Adventures

What's Under a Rock?

Time Is Short and the Water Rises
(with John Walsh)

Complete Book of Archery

The Motorless Flight Series

HALF MILE UP WITHOUT AN ENGINE

The Essentials, the Excitement of Sailplanes & Soaring

by Robert Gannon

Prentice-Hall, Inc., Englewood Cliffs, New Jersey 07632

Grateful acknowledgment is made to the following for permission to
reprint previously published material:

The Papers of Wilbur and Orville Wright, Marvin W. McFarland, Editor.
Copyright 1953 by the McGraw-Hill Book Company, Inc.
"On the Wings of the Wind," by Howard Siepen. Article published in
June 1929 issue of *National Geographic Magazine.*
The Glider Gang, by Milton Dank. Copyright © 1977 by Milton Dank.
The Complete Book of Sky Sports, by Linn Emrich. Copyright © 1970
by Linn Emrich. Published by The Macmillan Company.
Material consisting of description of soaring by Heinrich Dittmar,
from July 1938 issue of *National Geographic Magazine.*
Our Atmosphere, by Theo Loebsack, translated from the German by E. L. and
D. Rewald. Copyright © Biederstein Verlag GMBH, Muenchen, 1957; English
translation © William Collins Sons and Co., Ltd., London and Pantheon
Books Inc., New York, 1959; Pantheon Books, a Division of Random House, Inc.
"Frightening Experience During Jet-Stream Project," by Larry Edgar. Article
in July-August 1955 issue of *Soaring* magazine.
Various material in the Appendices provided by the Soaring Society of America.

*Half Mile Up Without an Engine: The Essentials,
the Excitement of Sailplanes & Soaring,* by Robert Gannon

Printed in the United States of America/Prentice-Hall International, Inc., London/Prentice-
Hall of Australia, Pty. Ltd., Sydney/Prentice-Hall of Canada, Ltd., Toronto/Prentice-Hall
of India Private Ltd., New Delhi/Prentice-Hall of Japan, Inc., Tokyo/Prentice-Hall of
Southeast Asia Pte. Ltd., Singapore/Whitehall Books Limited, Wellington, New Zealand

10   9   8   7   6   5   4   3   2   1

Library of Congress Cataloging in Publication Data

Gannon, Robert.
   Half mile up without an engine.
   (The Motorless flight series)
   Includes index.
   1. Gliding and soaring. I. Title. II. Series.
TL760.G29   629.132'31   81-12159
                        AACR2

ISBN 0-13-372169-8
ISBN 0-13-372151-5 {PBK.}

Contents

Preface

More than a decade ago, when I first took soaring lessons, I wrote this in an article that appeared in *Popular Science*:

> Now that the solo is over, let me tell you: Soaring is great. All the poetic talk that sailplane enthusiasts spout—about how the cares of the world dissipate, about feeling one with the plane, about the exhilaration and freedom and on-your-ownness—is all true. I know, because I, too, am now a sailplane nut.

Now, a dozen years later, I still am. As a contributing editor of *Popular Science*, I've tried a good number of the so-called solitary sports: rock climbing, scuba diving, dogsled racing, sky kiting, iceboating, parachuting—and I find that only soaring captures my continuing interest.

I'm not alone. In 1960 the Soaring Society of America had a membership of not many more than 3,000. By 1970 it had grown to nearly 11,000. By 1980,

16,000. And as of 1980, according to pilot Jon Mead, who has been looking into such statistics for the New England Soaring Council:

- Americans own about 3,000 gliders. That's about 500 more than the number of commercial airliners, and about twice as many as there are hot-air balloons.
- About 30,000 United States citizens are licensed to fly gliders.
- Americans soar for a total of about .25 million hours a year.

The kinds of people who soar are as varied as in any sport I can think of. They range from the physically superb, highly competitive athlete who vies for records and contest trophies to the person who is physically disabled and *can't* engage in any other active sport. From the teenager (the FAA allows fourteen-year-olds to solo) to the seventy-eight-year-old ex-master sergeant who says, "It's the only sport I know of in which you can seek your own level of risk." The physical requirements for soaring are almost nonexistent; no medical certificate is required to soar. A light person, in fact, has an advantage: Most sailplanes fly better with less weight in the cockpit.

The reasons for soaring vary as much as the participants. Two quotes: An airplane pilot soars on weekends because "power flight isn't fun anymore; the challenges are gone. It's the difference between a motorboat and sailboat; you just point the motorboat and go. In a sailplane, you're competing all the time against the elements." And a senior vice-president of one of the nation's largest banks bought his own sailplane because "you reach a point in life when the adventure stops. Soaring puts it back."

This book is designed to help you begin that adventure, whether you're a novice who has never stepped into a private plane or a power pilot deciding to add another rating.

To all the people who helped me put this book together, let me present a collective thanks. And a special note of gratitude to:

Tom Knauff, Doris Grove, Karl Striedieck, and Paul Schweizer for reading portions of the manuscript; Renee Jacobs, Rocky Miller, Dick Brown, Phil Dixon, and Mrs. Robert Symons for providing most of the photographs; Dolly Carr, Dave Witmer, and Martha Carothers for providing the line illustrations; the Camera Shop, State College, Pennsylvania, for the use of photographic equipment; Ned Owen, Carolyn Kerr, and Barbara Snow for acting as models; FAA examiner Sam Henry, who certified me for gliders, for being kind; the staff of the SSA for providing most of the data contained in the appendices; Saul Cohen for editing the book for Prentice-Hall; Cherene Holland for editorial guidance through various stages of the manuscript, and the Liberal Arts College Fund for Research, the Pennsylvania State University, for providing support.

I ended that first soaring article with this: "I look out of my window and see a cloud hanging, beckoningly, over the distant mountains and I long to spread my wings and get up under it to circle with the other hawks."

Let's.

Robert Gannon
Stormstown, Pennsylvania

Chapter One

Flight

With your left hand you reach out, grasp the golfball-size red knob, its shaft between your fingers, and as the altimeter needle slides over the 2,000-foot mark, you firmly pull. You hear a *thwunk* like something breaking (you're always somewhat surprised), and see the rope suddenly slither toward the towplane. Abruptly your sailplane's nose rises. You bank sharply to the right as the towplane, like a reverse mirror, dives off to the left.

Suddenly you let out a deep breath, a little surprised that you've been holding it. And as always, you get that *feeling*.

Power pilots don't know the feeling. They're working inside a *machine*—listening to the engine, monitoring the gauges, adjusting the mixture, watching rpm's and oil pressure and amps. Working. They're simply driving a means of transportation.

Scuba divers *do* understand, do recognize the feeling, and know it well. For a diver it comes after perhaps a dozen trips down, when he has become confident enough of his abilities to relax. Suddenly he feels as though he *belongs*. A swimmer never gets the feeling, of course. He's not in, he's *on* the water. Nor does the pilot of a submersible. Though fascinated, though enchanted with what's going on around him, he's nevertheless separated from the environment; he's only a rider, and he knows it. And a passenger in a jet, hermetically sealed, doesn't even come close. What he sees through the yellowing and greasy window is only a movie.

But a scuba diver, ah—he's at home, and in command. He needs but wave his hand and the whole world swivels. And a sailplane pilot, too, by simply moving his hand a few inches in any direction will cause the earth to shift.

The feeling, the crossover point, the sudden, amazing realization that you *belong* up there, for God's sake, in the *sky*—this emotional exhilaration that sometimes is so great you cry aloud—never comes during the training flights when the instructor is sitting behind. It makes no difference how many flights you've *handled* yourself; if your teacher comes along, that feeling doesn't. But you might very well experience it even on that first solo flight. The feeling might suddenly burst into your consciousness with the pull of the release knob—and that's why it's called that.

THWUNK! the towrope springs away like a silver cord, and suddenly you find yourself grinning, maybe even singing, maybe letting out little moans of pure joy—or at the very least talking to yourself, aloud. The Plexiglas bubble that surrounds you is so clean you forget it's there. You're out in the sky, and you're in command; you're not riding in a machine, you *are* that machine: Your arms reach out to end in wingtips, your little fingers the ailerons. Your legs may look like they're up there in front of you, but actually they're stretched behind, flowing into the rudder. You want to turn? Snugged into your shoulder harness you *will* yourself around, leaning your plane like a bicycle. You want to go faster? You *push* yourself.

And what do you do up there, wonder those who have never been there. It must be beautiful, they say; but don't you eventually get bored? they ask. What do you do?

You've got an awful lot to do, really; you're extraordinarily busy. It's work, but a peaceful kind of work—calm, with immediate rewards. No, not work—preoccupation.

The preoccupation with the flight starts on the runway, at the exact moment the towrope tightens, when abruptly the nose is jerked upright. Whatever you were worried about as you sat there depressed suddenly has recessed; the surge forward of your craft demands so much of your attention that there's none left for such trivialities as empty bank accounts and lost loves.

A glider circles up in a spiral unencumbered by an engine, guided only by rudimentary instruments and the pilot's sensitive touch. (Dick Brown, State College, PA)

Now the nose is bouncing around as you flounder at low speed, controls practically useless. But the air begins to flow faster over the surfaces, and with a last bounce the wheel leaves the turf. You're aloft. You want to haul back on that stick and get away from that ground quickly, but instead you hold the stick steady so that you skim the surface while the towplane, awkward bull that it is, begins to clamber into the sky through sheer horsepower.

And now you begin those great, winding, mile-wide spirals, higher and higher, flying in tandem with the towplane, following, mimicking, anticipating its sways and turns—rate of climb, 500 fpm; airspeed, 60. Easy, but you remember how hard it was in the beginning simply to follow: Your knuckles turned white and your jaw ached from clenching and your plane swung like a pendulum as you overreacted, sweeping farther and farther to the sides, zooming up and down, sometimes even passing through the towplane's vortices like a waterskier jumping wake. But that was all yesterday, and now you hardly give the technique a thought. Instead you're noting:

    —A *cu* over there, a cumulus cloud, just beginning to form;

    —Two hawks gently circling over there by the ridge;

    —The hint of a cloud bank off there in the distance, moving east.

All useful information for a birdman who'll soon be a mile up without an engine.

Two thousand feet. *Thwunk!* And the angry, disturbing, insulting internal-combustion growl follows the towplane down its spiral. In the relative quiet, you sigh.

Now, where was that cu? You ease the plane into a slow, smooth turn, getting your bearings, checking for other planes, deciding what you'll do first. You note that your rate-of-climb indicator, your *variometer*, is pointing downward, and that your altimeter now reads 1,800. Already you've lost 200 feet, and that just can't go on, so you head over toward the ridge, hoping that you'll find the wind rushing against it, hurdling it, strong enough to carry you aloft in the rising currents. Without lift of some sort, because your plane's glide ratio is 20:1—20 feet forward to 1 foot down—and because you're sinking at the rate of 180 fpm, you'll be down in another ten minutes or so, having glided (not soared, glided) less than eight miles. That mustn't be. You've got to find lift.

Off toward the ridge. But on the way, ha!—there's the underbelly of that cu, a midsize, billowy cloud maybe a half-mile away. That means that warm, moist air is thermaling up to become visible. You sail closer and suddenly you feel it—an almost subliminal jiggle, a gentle increase in airspeed like the first nibble on a fishline. Then again, as the left wing pulls upward ever so faintly. You wait a moment looking for . . . There it is; the *right* wing jiggles. That *was* the thermal, so you instantly stand on a wing to circle back in a tight, 300-foot hoop, and then you feel that gratifying *surge* upward as you penetrate the main lift, and for the second time this afternoon you grin, congratulating yourself on your sensitivity.

The variometer shows *up*. You're rising in a funnel of warm air, an expanding blob that a few minutes ago had formed, perhaps, on that newly plowed field of dark earth a mile or so upwind. Through the overhead canopy you watch the little cumulus cloud formed by the thermal. Slowly, circling around and around, you come closer to it, and now, at 4,200 feet, you're near enough to see the straggles of cotton wisping down from the sides, like lace smothered in fog. In the center, a dome of darker gray pushes up into the cloud, and you know that it is the portal for the main current of air, the best place for lift. You'd like to swing up into it, but you hold yourself back; the last time you did that you were swept right *into* the cloud—something not only illegal but frightening if you're not planning for it. So instead you just snuggle up under the cloud's refreshing coolness until, bit by bit, it begins to disintegrate. And your variometer edges over into the minus side again.

Of the four or five instruments before you, the variometer is the only one you're checking. At other times you must know your exact altitude, but today you can estimate close enough. And today, too, you can feel any slipping or sliding a lot more accurately than you can interpret the indicator. And when you land you must know your exact speed and keep it constant, but up here it doesn't really matter. You can guess close enough (too fast, too noisy; too slow, spookily quiet), and even if you forget and slow down so much that you stall, so what? You lose a few dozen feet. You do need your variometer, though, because at this height, unless a change is abrupt, you just can't tell if you are rising or sinking. So you rely on it. (Amateurs, in fact, often rely on it too much; they sometimes get so interested in watching the little pointer that they go into shock when they realize that the airport has drifted out of sight.)

Now as the cloud breaks up and the lift disappears, the arrow eases to the minus-200-feet-a-minute mark, your normal sink rate. Seems like a lot, but it's only a little more than a yard a second. You sink, and glide, and look for another thermal. None very close. So you head over to the ridge, to the hills or mountains running along the downwind side of the airport. You're looking now for ridge lift.

You check the ground to see if the wind is still blowing toward the ridge. Shadows of clouds tell you, at least, what's going on at 4,800 feet. Then you spot wood smoke coming from a chimney, rising at about a 30-degree angle and blowing toward the southeast, and that means that the wind is just fine for ridge lift.

So you swoop toward the ridge, and there, 300 feet from the side, is that hawk, still lazily floating. Soaring pilots use hawks almost as remote-sensing instruments. If you see a hawk circling, resting on his wings, you know that he's found uplift, and you can probably share it with him.

Your altimeter begins to wind clockwise again, reaches 1,600 feet, then stops, and holds there as you explore the ridge, mindful of the airport (you don't feel like off-landing in a farmer's cornfield today, although you've done it a few times before) as you soar back and forth.

And then you spot another little cu, edges sharp and crisp, as a young, still-forming cloud should look. It's close enough that you can sail over there, try it out for lift, and if it's weak scoot back to the ridge again. So you push your stick

Flight 5

forward to increase the speed, figure that if the cloud is *there*, the rising tube of air should slant up about *there*—and now *here*—but nothing. Did you miss it? Then suddenly you feel it, sail clean through, bank sharply back into it, and there you go up again. *This* is the thrill of soaring: discovering—and it's always an amazing revelation—discovering that without a motor you can actually climb the sky, that with a combination of the technology of your fine little aircraft and of your own judgment and skill, you can sail on and on and on.

The day is exciting, even though it's an easy flight, and even though you've done it a dozen, a hundred times before. On some flights you test yourself: You learn how to react to danger—to work for an hour in 30-knot winds to get enough height to return to base, then land at dusk; to clear treetops by 30 feet crossing the saddle of a mountain; to sneak up through a hole in the clouds that suddenly closes up, cutting you off from the earth.

But today, the easy flight. And eventually it ends. The sun no longer bakes loose thermals; the hawk must begin to flap his wings.

On your upwind leg you come in a little high, but you like the extra room. (You can always sink, but rise?) You throw your dive brakes on full, then as you near the ground, ease them down and slowly glide in a foot or two above the turf, pulling back, back, back on the stick until just as the wheel touches you stall. Perfect.

You bump to a halt, throw open the canopy, and once again sigh. You unbuckle your harness, but you don't get out. For a long moment you sit there, holding the magic, keeping the spell.

Chapter Two

From Daydreams to the Brothers Wright

It started way before the Wright brothers, back before Lilienthal, back before Leonardo, even—back, back to the time that man first began to have that recurrent dream of flying, of holding out his arms, pushing forward, lifting gently from the earth, and murmuring "It works." And the curiosity began to grow back when he first started to daydream. What would it be like, he wondered, to stretch out his arms, leap off a cliff, and glide like a hawk, *soar* like an eagle?

Those who tried it weren't very successful. Leaf through the records of history and you find dozens of figures fashioning wings with which to flap off across the valley. And that was their trouble: They tried to mimic the flappers instead of the soarers. The flights, often spectacular, were short.

Enter technology at the end of a string. Some centuries before Christ, an unknown, imaginative Chinese used some light rods to stiffen a fluttering banner. Then he allowed it, tethered, to blow away—and invented the kite. It wasn't too long before the concept was put to use as a signaling device. Around 1232, kites became the delivery mechanism for history's first air-leaflet raid: A provincial Chinese army flew propaganda-covered kites across the enemy's lines, then cut the strings.

A more exciting use for Chinese kites: man carriers. The passengers were observers—something like a tenth-century version of a spy satellite—but if there's one thing kite historians agree upon it's that nobody wanted the job. One reporter was Marco Polo, astonished to see Chinese sailors dangling from huge kites in the sky. He noted that the kites were outfitted with eight ropes for securing reluctant riders. "The men of the ship," he wrote in 1299, "will find someone stupid or drunken and will bind him on the hurdle; for no wise man nor undepraved would expose himself to that danger."

Some six hundred years later, Westerners began to lift themselves aloft on kites, and without even a war to impel them. Here, for example, is a translation of a letter that appeared in the French periodical *Le Cerf-volant* in 1910:

I read with interest your article on man-carrying kites, but I found no mention of Dr. Jules Laval of Dijon who, in 1854, made several experiments with a kite at least 10 metres high by 6 wide [33 x 20 feet], flown by four or five men. At the end of its tail it carried a little wickerwork chair, in which he got me to sit, holding on to me by means of a rope. At this time the kite was some 50 metres [164 feet] in the air.

The men were finding it very difficult to hold the kite down, and as they were getting rather near to the Suzon river they tied the line to an elder log which was lying behind a milestone at a turning in the road. Friction caused by the tension on the line caused the log to catch fire and the cord broke. I fell from a height of 9 or 10 metres [about 30 feet], but quite slowly and was not injured.

We returned home, and I have never again flown from a kite.

—H. Lieutet

In the meantime, airmen who were not maiming themselves doing kite dives were accomplishing the same thing with parachutes, patterned, according to one source, after falling leaves and thistledown. Leonardo da Vinci, of course, designed his own fifteenth-century version, a four-sided pyramid affair. It was never tried, although it probably would have worked if made large enough.

And Leonardo is credited with the first scientifically rational approach to aircraft design. He studied birds in flight, prepared an illustrated analysis of just what happens, then speculated on how man could duplicate it. He would have failed, just as the others before him failed, because he concentrated on flying rather than gliding. Had he focused on bird *aeronautics* instead of anatomy, and

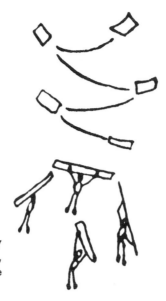

Leonardo da Vinci's sketch is probably the first of his studies of gliding flight, and a precursor to his invention of the parachute.

had he forgotten about such distractions as Mona Lisa and the Last Supper, he very likely would have become the first person to soar. He could not have developed powered flight, but he had all the materials at his disposal to build a sailplane.

He didn't fly, but he did influence the future of flight. What he did was to show the world that someone other than a lunatic was actually considering the possibility of man *flying*—a concept that today would be about on a par with levitation through meditation. Leonardo was a person of stature, and here he thought flying was a real possibility. Staggering. His theories sparked the beginning of serious aeronautical research.

For the next three hundred years, though, the spark served mainly to lead to disaster. One attempt that could be classified as either disaster or wild success, depending on your perspective, was the famous mid-1800s flight piloted by a salt- and sun-dazed French sea captain named Jean Marie La Bris. He had spent so many years watching seabirds glide that eventually he convinced himself that he could do the same. So he put together a tow-line glider that looked like an albatross, and hired a horse-drawn carriage to pull it. The plan was that he'd squat inside the bird, shouting commands to the coachman, and, as it began to lift, try to control the wings with levers that varied their inclination.

Surprisingly, it worked. Unfortunately, the horse took one look at this gargantuan bird rising behind him and bolted. The towrope broke. Then the rope snagged the driver. And he spiraled aloft 300 feet, hollering all the way.

La Bris was ecstatic. The coachman was not. But at least the contraption flew. Most other birdmen of the day would fashion themselves wings of peeled willow rods covered with waxed fabric, strap the appendages onto their backs, then go galloping down a hill or off a cliff, flapping like crazy. Most were killed, of course.

About the same time as La Bris took to the air, gliders were being developed by Sir George Cayley, who lived near Scarsborough, England. And it is Cayley who is generally recognized as *the* inventor of aircraft. Some of his insights were truly amazing, and if other technicians had followed in his footsteps, the age of flight could have dawned scores of years sooner. He recognized, for example, the value of dihedral—the upward inclination of the wing—for stability. He saw the usefulness of a "weathervaning" tail assembly mounted behind the wing, again for stability, like feathers on an arrow. And he discovered the need for a cambered airfoil—a wing with a top surface more rounded than the bottom—for maximum lift (see Chapter Five).

He had confidence in his designs, but apparently not enough to try them out himself. He did, however, give rides to local dogs and goats, and to at least one ten-year-old boy. And then in 1852 Cayley talked his coachman, John Appleby, into taking a ride. (Apparently the mid-eighteen-hundreds produced a surplus of coachmen.) His current airplane model looked like a boat with two bicycle wheels in front and a smaller one behind, and above spread a wing of fabric stretched out on Erector Set girders. Launch site was a cliff that towered above a valley near Brompton Hall, Yorkshire.

The servant looked over the edge just once and declared that he'd changed his mind about the whole thing. But by then it was too late; Cayley was already tilting the contraption, and along with the terrified servant it slid off into space. They began to plummet, then the wings caught the air, and they sailed, porpoising gently across the valley. A beautiful flight.

The landing wasn't. The glider smashed into the turf, demolishing on impact. Unharmed, the world's first aviator brushed himself off, looked across to his launching site, quit his coachman position, and fled into obscurity.

Next: Otto Lilienthal, second only to the Wright brothers in the awe with which soarers hold him. He was a wild-eyed Pomeranian who, in 1889, wrote what the Smithsonian calls "perhaps the most important book published during the nineteenth century on the subject of aviation": *Der Vogelflug als Grundlage der Flieebkunst* (*Birdflight as the Basis of Aviation*). It describes the results of a massive series of tests designed to extend Cayley's theories by probing the reasons that birds can fly, including detailed analyses of the lift created by curved surfaces in moving air.

He applied the principles to eighteen gliders built between 1891 and 1896, and launched from his own, homebuilt, 50-foot hill. Some worked, some didn't, but all looked pretty much like replacement parts for a Burmese bridge.

Otto Lilienthal displays his biplane glider, just outside Berlin . . . (Smithsonian Institution Photo No. A48093E)

. . . then tests it, gliding from the slope of a hill. (Smithsonian Institution Photo No. 73-3022)

Lilienthal would crawl under a cotton-covered, willow-and-bamboo-frame glider, lift up its 44 pounds, then run like mad into the wind or off the brow of his hill until he was airborne, hanging from parallel bars under his armpits, controlling the flight (sometimes for up to 900 feet) by swinging his dangling legs, and eventually (at least in theory) landing on his feet. He made some 2,000 flights, and he learned to turn and to some extent to use air currents to extend flights.

Eventually he was killed. One day he was gliding down a slope when a gust of wind zipped him up to 50 feet. The wind died, the plane stalled, and Lilienthal, in his eighteenth glider model, clumped to earth.

With Lilienthal dead, the world's aeronautical attention shifted to a Lenin lookalike named Octave Chanute, one of the most successful civil engineers in America. Bored with bridges and railroads, Chanute retired in 1889 as chief engineer for the Erie Railroad and turned exclusively to flight. He believed that to develop a practical powered aircraft, a successful *glider* had first to be built. He put together a multitude of them, then flew them at his test facilities along the sand-dune shore of Lake Michigan near Miller, Indiana. Chanute was more than an engineer; he was an organizer, a clearinghouse of information, a historian, and a financial supporter of research.

In his sixties by then, he decided that he was just too old to do much testing himself, so he hired Augustus M. Herring. Herring had studied mechanical engineering at Stevens Institute of Technology for four years, but failed to graduate. His thesis proposal, "The Heavier Than Air Flying Machine as a Mechanical Engineering Problem," was rejected as fanciful—and as a result he lost interest in formal education. Instead, he bought one of Lilienthal's monoplane "standard gliders" for 600 marks, and built at least one glider (probably more) of his own design, which, he reported later, failed. After working for a time with Samuel Langley, secretary of the Smithsonian Institution, he joined Chanute as a part-time pilot, part-time engineer.

The first designs they tried were copied largely from Lilienthal's plans. But soon Chanute realized that the technique of using acrobatic swings of the body to compensate for wind gusts (the cause of Lilienthal's death) was hardly satisfactory. Some sort of automatic control—built-in stability—was necessary. "The machine should be so constructed," he said, "that the position of the center of gravity would give the apparatus a downward inclination. With such a machine one would circle like a bird, rise spirally like a bird, and soar in any direction." And the thinking led to such developments as a shiftable center of gravity, a stabilizing, vertical tail, and cambered wings. The plane most identified with the two men is known as the "standard" biplane glider, a craft that weighed only 32 pounds—less than a single cement block—yet it carried Herring as far as 360 feet.

Octave Chanute's 1897 glider is carried up an Indiana dune . . . (Smithsonian Institution Photo No. 30908L)

. . . and is flown down again by Augustus Herring. (Smithsonian Institution Photo No. A48095L)

Modern-day equivalent of nineteenth-century glider is the Quadruplane, designed by Larry Hall of Morgan, Utah. His idea was to "put a little bit of myself on each of several small gliders and fly them all in formation."

14 **From Daydreams to the Brothers Wright**

So stable were the Chanute designs to become that Herring was able to make some flights in winds exceeding 30 mph. Eventually he learned to turn the plane so that it flew *lengthwise* along the hillsides, and he found that he could stay up longer, and sometimes even rise above the takeoff site; this was the discovery of ridge lift. In October 1896 Herring established a new world record: 48 seconds in a flight that covered 927 feet.

Chanute was innovative, driving, rational, and inventive, and he had money to back his schemes. He designed a whole series of gliders and ran them through thousands of flights. His biplane was the most advanced craft in the world; compared with all the others, it was safe, reliable, easy to handle. And yet his designs were not all that important to the future of aviation. What *was* important, his main contribution to the field of aeronautics, was really rather dull: his support of the Wright brothers.

And the Wrights, in the space of a single year, simultaneously perfected the elementary glider and nearly destroyed it.

Chapter Three

Kitty Hawk and Beyond

Suddenly, when on that December 17 afternoon in 1903 Orville Wright's new engine-powered aircraft flew him into immortality, the world ceased to care a whit about motorless flight. Throughout the years at Kitty Hawk the brothers' drive was always toward powered aircraft; gliders were only steppingstones. Nevertheless, Wilbur was constantly enchanted by the idea of soaring and, one suspects, accepted its apparent demise with reluctance. Many an afternoon he would trudge off across the dunes to find a spot from which he could watch hawks in flight, meticulously recording their engineering. For example, here are some jottings from his notebook:

The buzzard which uses the dihedral angle finds greater difficulty to maintain equilibrium in strong winds than the eagles and hawks which hold their wings level.

The hen hawk can rise faster than the buzzard and its motion is steadier. It displays less effort in maintaining its balance.

A damp day is unfavorable for soaring unless there is a high wind.

No bird soars in a calm.

The bird certainly twists its wing tips so that the wind strikes one wing on its top and the other on its lower side, thus by force changing the bird's lateral position.

Birds cannot soar to leeward of a descending slope unless high in the air.

And when Orville, in 1920, looked back at his and Wilbur's work over the last two decades, he remembered this as the reason for beginning to pursue the fanciful notion of flight in the first place:

In the Spring of the year 1899 our interest in the subject was again aroused through the reading of a book on ornithology. We could not understand that there was anything about a bird that would enable it to fly that could not be built on a larger scale and used by man. At this time our thought pertained more particularly to gliding flight and soaring. If the bird's wings would sustain it in the air without the use of muscular effort, we did not see why man could not be sustained by the same means.

The first time their interest was prodded was in 1895, when they first began to read about Otto Lilienthal's work. Then, next year, when they read in the Dayton newspaper of Lilienthal's death, they became so enchanted with his experiments, and so startled that they had ended, that they decided to carry on where he had left off. As they discussed it, though, they concluded that they should approach the basic design from another angle. Lilienthal's big mistake, they thought, was that he had attempted to control the aircraft's flight by having the pilot swing his legs around to shift the center of gravity. In a 1900 letter to Octave Chanute, Wilbur expanded: "I . . . conceive Lilienthal's apparatus to be inadequate not only from the fact that he failed, but my observations of the flight of birds convince me that birds use more positive and energetic methods of regaining equilibrium than that of shifting the center of gravity."

In the same letter, Wilbur also pointed out the small amount of flight time that Lilienthal had managed to build up over all his years of experimentation: "The fact that in five years' time he spent only about five hours altogether in actual flight," wrote Wilbur, "is sufficient to show that his method was inadequate. Even the simplest intellectual or acrobatic feats could never be learned with so short practice."

Wilbur also asked Chanute for ideas on where he and Orville could experiment—someplace with winds that would be suitable for experiments. Chanute suggested the Atlantic coast, somewhere around the Carolinas or Georgia. The Wrights then found out specifics from the National Weather

Bureau, and finally, with the help of the local postmaster, selected a mosquito- and sand flea-laden site near the hamlet of Kitty Hawk, North Carolina.

Then, in Dayton, they got to work. First, they eliminated Lilienthal's dangling legs. Instead, using Chanute's biplane as their model, they developed a design that would allow the pilot to lie facedown on the lower wing. Such a position would not only reduce drag but would obviate the absurd necessity of the pilot having to land on his own feet—and all subsequent sailplane pilots have been grateful.

Second, because steering by shifting body weight was decidedly inefficient, they eliminated the birdlike tail that every plane up to that time had sticking out behind, and they moved it up front where they could see it and better control it. Then they added an elevator to it. Third (and this, according to modern aeronautical engineers, was the Wrights' single most important contribution to flight), they arranged a method of *warping* the wings during flight—a forerunner of ailerons—to control lateral stability. Now if a gust of wind knocked a plane off course, the pilot would slightly warp a wing, the plane would roll a bit, then more or less *lift itself* around the turn back to the right course again.

They built separate parts of the weird-looking craft in Dayton (for about $15), then toted them to Kitty Hawk for assembly. The finished, 52-pound biplane (each wing 18 by 5 feet) was largely of ash covered with white French sateen. That first summer they flew it as a kite for a total of barely ten minutes, and as a glider for only about two minutes. Nevertheless, they felt that they had proved their theory: Warping the wings was better than shifting the weight of the pilot.

At the end of the summer the brothers went back home, and then in 1901 returned with a new and improved version, the wings 22 by 7 feet—the biggest machine anyone had ever tried to fly. The plane was controllable, but they discovered that much of the basic research done by Chanute, Lilienthal, and the rest was worthless, that if they were to proceed they'd have to begin with the basics, a formidable undertaking. Said Wilbur on the way back to Ohio: It would be a thousand years before man would fly.

It was then that Chanute performed his greatest service to the field of aviation. He talked the brothers into continuing with their dream. They put together the world's first wind tunnel—16 inches across and 6 feet long—tested some 200 tiny wings in it, then built a scale model of a wholly new plane, tested it, and began to disprove the old figures one by one. Orville himself, looking back on the work from the perspective of 1919, wrote, "Our experiences in 1901 proved conclusively to us that the tables of air pressure then in existence were entirely unreliable. . . . It was really [the wind tunnel] work that made possible the construction of our first power flyer." Without that wind tunnel, most aeronautical historians now believe, flight probably would have been postponed for a half century or more.

In the fall of 1902 they traveled back once more to the Kitty Hawk dunes, this time lugging the largest glider ever: a 32-foot-wingspread monster that weighed a massive 116 pounds, wringing wet. The tail had returned to the rear end, and to help with the roll problem, the brothers had added a vertical stabilizer.

Satisfied, finally, that they had a plane that *could* fly, now they had to learn *how* to fly it. First, they glided with the elevator locked flat, using wing-warping devices alone—again and again and again. When they finally felt that they knew exactly how those control surfaces affected performance in all manner of winds, they added the elevator, and over the next couple of hundred flights concentrated on using both sets of controls at the same time (to make what they called "coordinated turns") in winds of up to 36 mph.

The plane was still not working exactly as they wanted. Whenever they would bank in an attempt to turn, the nose would cantankerously slide over, pointing in the wrong direction before gradually coming around again. They had discovered "aileron drag" (see Chapter Five), and they solved it by replacing the rear half of the vertical stabilizer with a section that moved, a flap they could waggle when they pushed on pedals. They called it a rudder, and with that addition had developed a craft that even a modern-day glider pilot would find mildly comfortable.

Altogether that summer the Wrights made nearly a thousand flights. And they flew knowing that their glider had few of the hazards that killed so many experimenters before them. All of the flights were less than about a half minute, and none stretched to much more than about 600 feet—considerably shorter than even the records of that day. But the Wrights weren't interested in distance or time-aloft competition; they cared only about research.

That was the summer of 1902. Now they were satisfied that (1) they knew how to fly, and (2) they had a machine that *could* fly. And so they had time, over the winter, to develop an engine for the plane. The next winter, on a cold December 17, they flew it.

And nearly killed the sport of gliding.

A few stunts briefly revived interest—the flights of John J. Montgomery, for instance. He was a Californian who had been quietly working on gliders near the Mexican border, and who claimed to have made 600-foot flights there as early as 1883, even before Lilienthal. Later he launched his gliders from balloons at 4,000 feet, and the newspapers temporarily went wild. Then he, too, was forgotten.

The Wrights, meanwhile, had established a world record—but again, nobody cared. While testing a new stabilizer in 1911, Orville soared across the Kitty Hawk dunes for 9 minutes, 45 seconds. The record would stand for years.

PIONEERS OF MOTORLESS FLIGHT

1250	Unknown	Short-lived passengers on Chinese observation kites.
1850s	Dr. Jules Laval	French experimenter with man-carrying kites.
1850s	Jean Marie La Bris	First towline glider.
1850s	Sir George Cayley	Recognized as glider's inventor; developer of dihedral and cambered airfoil.
1883 (?)	John Montgomery	Probably first controlled flight.
1890s	Otto Lilienthal	German aviation writer and inventor who made eighteen glider models.
1890s	Octave Chanute	American engineer who, with pilot A. M. Herring, formulated principles of stability and developed the "standard biplane." Discovered ridge lift. Made about 7,000 flights.
1894	Charles Steinmetz and friends	Founded world's first glider club, the Mohawk Aerial Navigation Company, in Schenectady, New York.
1900s	Wright brothers	Perfected controls. In 1903, first power flight.

Later, in 1919, reviewing their work, Orville, just as he had done so many years before, was thinking mainly about birds.

Our early experiments at Kitty Hawk [he wrote] were conducted for the purpose of developing a method of maintaining equilibrium in the air and also to learn something about soaring flight. . . .

We had the opportunity of witnessing daily the soaring flight of buzzards, fish and chick hawks, and eagles. Attempts to imitate their flight without a motor have not been very successful, although in 1902 and 1903 we made a dozen or more flights in which we remained in the air for more than a minute with no, or scarcely any, descent; and in 1911 Mr. Alec Ogilvie and I continued the soaring experiments at Kitty Hawk and succeeded in making a number of flights of more than five minutes' duration . . . without loss of any height at all. In many cases we landed at a higher point than the one from which we started. I see no reason why flights of several hours' duration cannot be made without the use of a motor. But, of course, these flights must be made in rising trends of air—a condition required by all birds for soaring flight.

That 1911 world-record run of less than ten minutes doesn't sound very impressive, and it wasn't even to Orville; he simply wanted to try out a new stabilizer, and a long gliding flight was the best way. The record lasted for ten years mainly because nobody tried to break it. Gliders, it seemed, would remain only a developmental step in aviation history.

They probably would have disappeared entirely had it not been for World War I, and for Germany's use of the new invention, the airplane, as a weapon. At the end of the war, to ensure that the German war machine, including the threat of a dreaded Luftwaffe, would never rise again, the Treaty of Versailles was instituted. It forbade Germany to build submarines, tanks, or military aircraft. *Military*, of course, meant planes with engines. Planes *without* were toys, of course—or at most, sports equipment. And the boys who subsequently learned to fly the gliders—eventually some 200,000 by one count (a thousand times the United States number) were encouraged simply because of the sport of it. Of course. The fact is, happenstance or not, when in 1935 Chancellor Hitler unilaterally declared the Treaty of Versailles to be null and void, the Third Reich had more pilots than any other country in the world.

Politics aside, to be a German schoolboy in the nineteen-twenties and thirties was exciting; you *learned to fly*. Any boy fourteen years or over in the republic could enroll, and it didn't cost him a pfennig. The potential pilots learned quickly, too. Had to; the very first time a student slipped into the hard leather seat of a glider, he took hold of the controls, slipped off into space, and *soloed*. No dual training then; either you performed satisfactorily the first time or you might never get a second chance. When you finally learned how to fly, you really *knew*. Those young Germans learned more about flying—about weather conditions, about controls, about what air does when it runs over the surface of a flying machine—than perhaps most power pilots do even today.

The Germans were serious. In 1920, less than eighteen months after the Armistice was signed, Germany held the world's first glider meet, a two-week affair. A year later, at the next meet, the Germans broke Orville Wright's duration flight three times in two weeks. In the eleven months between the meets they had delineated gliding and soaring, and they did so dramatically. First, a pilot named Wolf Hirth, in a Harth-Messerschmitt glider, attacked the time-aloft record and demolished it by flying for twenty-two minutes. (By the next year records would be measured by *hours*.) Next, his friend Wolfgang Klemperer rose to 6,000 feet on one flight, and then later outdid himself by completing the world's first cross-country flight to an announced destination. He flew three miles in about fifteen minutes, and that was the first solid proof that the direction a motorless plane took could actually be controlled by its pilot.

By that time the Germans had established the world capital of soaring at Mount Wasserkuppe, in the Rhön Mountains, and even today ex-Luftwaffe pilots journey back there to sing the old songs with nostalgia.

Meanwhile, away from the schools, designers were turning gliders into sailplanes. Biwings were disappearing, and sleeker, enclosed bodies were developed as the engineers discovered streamlining. Wings grew to 60 feet, even more, to provide lower rates of sink.

Pilots were becoming more aware of meteorology, too. They began to notice that often when puffy white cumulus clouds drifted over their hillsides, they would be able to climb to greater heights. Early experimenters dreaded gusts, squalls, and clouds, but now pilots were deliberately leaving their safe ridge-lift areas to seek them out, to look for those strange updrafts. Soon soarers became free of the hills and the wind. From then on they hop-skipped from cloud to cloud; cross-country flying had begun. Here's how Wolf Hirth, in a 1929 *National Geographic* article, described a cross-country Rhön flight.

From a hilltop of the Wasserkuppe I shot off into space like a torpedo, by using . . . a "slope upward" air stream. Low clouds were near and in a few turns I was among them. Silent as a ghost, I slipped through the gray, wet clouds. With a soft breeze against my tail, I floated gently with a feeling of utter detachment from all earthy things. . . .

But in my drift through the clouds I had lost much height. So much, in fact, that though I cruised along the mountain slopes I not only failed to gain height, but was near-ly forced down. My tail-skid was actually scraping through the grass of a meadow when the upcurrent from a tiny break in the mountain slope threw me suddenly more than 90 feet straight up into the air! An "air bump," aviators would call that current. But it kindly gave me enough elevation to go on over that mountain slope. Here a group of boys, herding some cows, came running up as my skid swept the grass, hoping to see me land. But again I took the air, probably to their youthful disappointment.

Cruising easily about for half an hour, I again found myself high in the clouds. Once more the dense, white mists folded about me. With no instruments aboard, I turned my plane to the wind, feeling for its direction and strength. But I must have banked too steeply on the curve. A quick, powerful gust hit me unexpectedly and, in a split second, I was floundering helplessly in the most dangerous situation of all my flying career.

Now the air fairly roared past—and I was falling! I pulled the elevator up, but only felt the wind tearing faster past my sides. In the next instant I fell out of the clouds, with one wing down, in a dizzy sideslip.

But once below the clouds, I could see the ground again and judge the position of my plane. Quick, gentle pressure on the rudder and I was righted, on an even keel. . . .

But by this time I had again lost much altitude. In the [Saale] river valley lay the hamlet of Steinach. I cruised low over it. My sudden, silent appearance just over their heads greatly astonished the inhabitants. They came running out into the road to see me land. But I had to disappoint them, too. By cruising steadily back and forth along the slope where the ruined Steinach Castle stands, I worked up high again. . . .

Following the broad Saale Valley, circling repeatedly over favorable slopes to gain height, I crossed over the villages of Bocklet and Grossenbrach. Then . . . I discovered in front of me the famous resort town of Kissingen. Near it was a large airdrome. A good place to light! But when I saw mountains stretching along the outskirts of the town, I decided to stay up and risk flying across Kissingen.

I was lucky enough to make it. Fifty yards over the railway depot I could not resist playing the role of the "air ghost," as on previous similar occasions. I shouted "Hello there!" at the top of my voice. Passengers waiting on the platform for their train, startled by the shout from the skies, stared up in amazement.

From slope to slope, across roads and forests, I flew; then along a railway, creeping up valley. I knew I would not be able to continue much longer, but tried to cover as many miles as possible. On the left and on the right of the road and railway to Schweinfurt below me, two mountain ranges now came together in an acute angle. The northwest wind blew straight into this corner and I was caught as in a trap.

Then an upward air stream lifted me so high that I could fly along the saddle and glide down gradually over the plain that lay behind. A motor car was just coming along the road. Here was a chance to reach a telephone. So I flew over the car, made a sharp curve, and landed smoothly 60 feet from the road, on a meadow. The driver took me to the next village, and ten minutes after my landing, the competition management on the Wasserkuppe knew of my whereabouts.

Later, with the heavier reliance on thermals (they called it "cloud-lift" then), planes changed even more quickly than in the early years. Now to stay inside the rising air column, the aircraft had to be agile and quick. With ridge soaring (Hirth's "slope-upwind") the important thing was to have a low rate of sink; with thermaling, the most important thing was to be able to travel distances at flat glide angles, so that the search for the next thermal could be extended. At the 1926 Wasserkuppe meet, a pilot named Max Kegal flew up near the base of a thunderhead and was suddenly sucked up into it. Before he could get down again he not only had broken the altitude record but had doubled the previous distance record.

Now pilots were landing in unexpected areas, and so their machines had to be strengthened. Spot landings became more important, so spoilers and dive brakes—devices to enable the plane quickly to lose altitude—were developed. And all the time the glide ratio—the relationship between the distance covered to height lost—was being extended. By the outbreak of World War II, the best sailplanes had glide ratios of 30:1, or 30 feet forward for every foot lost in altitude.

In the meantime, by the end of the nineteen-twenties, Germany was home to 200 glider clubs, and in the annual competitions usually more than a hundred machines were entered. Americans could hardly have cared less. Although back in 1922 a glider designed and built by MIT students had been piloted by Eddie Allen at a meet at the Wasserkuppe, that was the only try at competition.

And then in 1928 a group of German pilots were checking out Cape Cod for soaring conditions, when one of them, Peter Hesselbach, startled American pilots by staying aloft for more than four hours—an unofficial United States endurance record—sailing back and forth above the breakers. Now the Yankees were interested, and almost immediately the American Motorless Aviation Corporation, the country's first gliding school, was formed at South Wellfleet, Cape Cod, and outfitted with German gliders and German instructors.

Other interests surfaced. In fact, America, in 1930, seemed to be trying to make up for lost time:

Item: The first national contest was held at Elmira, New York, a site selected by the same Wolfgang Klemperer who performed such surprising feats back on the Wasserkuppe.

Item: The National Glider Association was organized in Detroit by, among others, W. B. Mayo, chief engineer of the Ford Motor Company; Klemperer, who by now was an engineer for the Goodyear Zeppelin Co., of Akron; and Amelia Earhart. * The members reflected aviation interests who saw the cheap, easy-to-fly *primary* glider as a neat way to get potential customers interested in power planes.

Item: The so-called utility glider, the Franklin PS-2, was introduced—single-wheeled, rugged, yet fairly high in performance. It became the mainstay of U.S. gliding.

Item: A glider flown by U.S. Navyman Ralph Barnaby (who first flew in his home-built Lilienthal glider in 1909) was dropped from the Navy blimp U.S.S. *Los Angeles.*

Item: Frank Hawks, in a Franklin Eaglet, was towed by a Waco biplane from California to New York.

Item: Both Charles and Anne Lindbergh took up soaring.

Item: Dozens of glider clubs and glider manufacturers popped up across the country. And perhaps most important of all, three brothers named Schweizer, using photos from that same 1929 *National Geographic* article, built a glider in their father's barn—and anyone who soars in America today is in their debt.

And it all happened in 1930.

---

* Among the other organizers of the NGA: Dr. Peter Altman and Hawley Bowlus (who had worked on Lindbergh's *Spirit of St. Louis*), both directors of NGA; Charles F. Kettering, of General Motors; Admiral W. A. Moffett; General J. F. O'Ryan; Bill Stout; Charles Lawrence; Eddie Stinson, of the Stinson Airplane firm; and Eddie Rickenbacker.

The Schweizer brothers, Paul, Ernest, and William, pose in 1960 at their Elmira factory. Later that year, Paul captained the U.S.A. soaring team, which competed at the World's Gliding Championships in Cologne, Germany. (Schweizer Aircraft)

THE SCHWEIZERS THREE

On the nineteenth of June 1930, three brothers named Schweizer opened the door of their father's barn, threw back a bedspread that had been hiding their home-built glider, and with the help of a dozen kids from around the neighborhood, carefully hauled the contraption to the top of a nearby rise.

They had been secretly working on it for six months. Ernest, eighteen, was the designer, getting his inspiration mainly from photographs of the German *Zoegling* illustrated in a 1929 *National Geographic* article. The work was secret, recalls Ernest, because "Papa wasn't very sympathetic with our project. He couldn't even drive a nail." The secret was easy to keep. The father was the chef at the old Carnegie Hall Restaurant, and because the trip from Peekskill to Manhattan was lengthy, he was away from home much of the time. And fortunately, when he was home, he didn't go into the barn very often.

Up on that rise, Paul, fifteen, slid onto the bicycle seat that served as the cockpit; Will, eleven, steadied the craft as best he could; and Ernie hooked shock cords—5/8-inch elastic ropes made of rubber straps bound together in woven cases—to the front, and directed the operation. Three of the young onlookers then sat on the ground, holding the glider back, while most of the rest stretched the cords out in front nearly to double their lengths.

"Okay—now!" said Ernie. The plane rushed forward, the cord stretchers fled to the sides, and Paul, not quite terrified, rose from the ground to an altitude of nearly a foot. "Hardly a record-breaking flight," recalled Paul almost exactly fifty years later, "but the darn thing *flew*, and I think that all of us were a bit surprised."

The brothers were so pleased with their success that they began to devote almost all of their time to gliding, and soon they found themselves receiving orders to build planes for others. In 1935 they formed the Schweizer Metal Aircraft Company to produce gliders commercially.

In the meantime, they were attending the periodic contests being held on Elmira's Harris Hill. Then, after the two older Schweizers had received their degrees in aeronautical engineering, they moved the whole operation to the Glider Capital of America, as Elmira had begun calling itself, after "Wasserkuppe West" failed to catch on.

Then came World War II. The United States Air Corps saw the need for training gliders, and the Schweizers were all set up to supply them. All told, the company produced about 200 TG-2s and TG-3s.

The war ended, the pilots came home, and the Schweizer employees—who, in the meantime, had developed some grand new high-performance models—stood waiting for the sailplane boom. They had a long wait. All those military training gliders came back to haunt them. "We thought there was going to be a big, unlimited market," says Paul. "We didn't anticipate the glut, the impact of all those gliders that we had built. They were being sold for $200 or $300 as war surplus. They did spread soaring—but they practically eliminated our market."

The company continued to fabricate parts for power-plane manufacturers—for Republic, Piper, Bell, Fairchild, and others (and built more than two thousand complete Grumman AG-Cat crop dusters)—and gradually moved back into the sailplane business again as those old gliders, oh so slowly, disappeared.

Today, sailplane manufacturing is still the smaller part of the business, but Schweizer remains by far the biggest glider manufacturer outside Europe, and so far has built more than 2,200 civilian sailplanes in 15 models.

Schweizer Aircraft factory and its affiliated soaring school, adjacent to the Chemung (New York) County Airport. (Schweizer Aircraft)

The nineteen-thirties continued, and the history of gliders in America was punctuated by the 1932 founding of the Soaring Society of America (with Warren E. Eaton, a World War I combat pilot, as its first president), by mail delivery in 1934 (a three-glider train, hauled by a towplane, dropped off mail-filled gliders in Philadelphia, Baltimore, and Washington, D.C.), by the first issue of *Soaring* in 1937. All over America youngsters were following plans appearing in *Popular Science* and *Popular Mechanics* and building primaries—little more than a trussed, open fuselage supporting wings, tail surfaces, and the pilot. Students who survived the *primary* graduated to the *secondary*—enclosed, with longer wings and better performance—and then combined the two in their third plane, a *utility*. (The Schweizer 2-33 design is a direct descendant of the utility.)

In the meantime, events were taking place in Germany that were not exactly sporting. Suddenly, things were getting serious. Where planes once were flung into the air with catapulting cords for exhilarating, free-flight climbs into thermals, now glider trains were crisscrossing the *Vaterland* in an intense national effort to train pilots in towing technique. And the aircraft themselves were undergoing change, too, almost reversing history: They were being transformed from sailplanes back to gliders. At one point Hermann Goering, destined to become commander of the Luftwaffe, in what has since been described as an "unguarded moment," mentioned in 1922 to America's World War I hero Eddie Rickenbacker that if the pre-Armistice German republic was ever to be "recaptured," it would be done through air power—and then, a minute later, he was talking about the German policy of teaching the sport of gliding to German youth.

By the mid-nineteen-thirties Germany had developed a glider large enough to carry weather equipment and two meteorologists, along with the pilot. The craft was called a flying observatory (OBS), and it was excellent for studying weather patterns; without an engine its flight was vibrationless and quiet, with no electrical noise to interfere with delicate equipment. But one day at the Munich airport, Hitler saw the plane, and he visualized it full not of meteorologic equipment but of troops. Not long afterward, he enlisted the guidance of General Ernst Udet, a World War I fighter pilot, and by 1937, the OBS, modified and enlarged, had become the combat-ready DFS-230 transport glider.

Until May 11, 1940, most of the world continued to think that those nice German glider boys were simply sports enthusiasts. But that was the date of history's first airborne assault. The objective: Belgium's Fort Eben Emael, a gigantic fortress near the German border, blasted out of solid rock, and thought to be impregnable. Silently, at dawn, in ten DFS-230s, 78 German glider troops settled behind the massive walls, onto the 5-foot-thick grass roof. In fifteen minutes they had nullified the 850 defenders and had blown up the only real fortification between the German border and Paris, with a loss of only six men.

Not surprisingly, this piqued the interest of the U.S. military, who, in typical American overkill fashion, reacted by producing in the next few years 14,000 combat gliders. (At one point they were planning to build two and a half times that many.) Gliders were desirable because they were cheap, silent, and efficient; an airplane could haul gliders carrying three times as many men as it could carry alone. And commanders didn't even have to teach the troops to pack parachutes.

The gliders varied in design from two-place trainers to the British Hamilcar, large enough to transport the Tetrarch tank. But because they were all gliders, not sailplanes, with a maximum 10:1 glide ratio (as opposed to some of today's sailplanes with glide ratios passing 50:1), they landed with sort of a thud—that is, if, during the slow trip to the combat zone, they got through the weather and flak at all. "They were dropped into the sea off Sicily, scattered at night over Normandy, and released over a thick smoke screen across the Rhine," says Milton Dank in *The Glider Gang*. Who were the pilots? Again, Dank: "Flunked-out aviation cadets; men who were too old for flight-crew training or who could not pass the strict physical examination; ground troops who wished to get into the Air Corps; men who wanted adventure, wanted to try something new—and, above all, to fly."

The last German assault using gliders was against the Aegean island of Crete. Seventy-five DFS-230s carried more than 700 largely airsick men plus ammunition, mortars, and even bicycles, and tried to land amid the craggy mountains. They crash-landed in dry riverbeds, on rocky mountain slopes, on country roads, and in trees, spilling men and equipment in their wake. Paratroops who followed fared little better, and the combined disaster convinced Hitler to drop plans for future airborne assaults: "The initial success was a result of surprise," he said, "and now the surprise is gone." Neither paratroops nor gliders were ever again used by the Germans in a major airborne role.

The Allies took up the slack with little better success. One typical assault took place on the night of July 9, 1943, when planes towed 136 American Wacos and 8 British Morsas from North Africa to the waters off southern Sicily (through flak from Allied destroyers), then cut them loose at 1,900 feet to attempt to put down on some of the most unlikely landing areas imaginable. At night. Under heavy fire. With winds blowing at gale force. Few of the pilots were familiar with these kinds of gliders, and none had flown at night more than once or twice.

Sixty-nine Wacos landed in the sea. Ten craft simply disappeared. And only four of the gliders that had set out were able to find their designated landing zones.

As the first and last war ever to use gliders ground to a stop, Congress, taking a page from prewar Germany's book, decided that one way to keep the American guard up was through gliders. The solution, according to a House resolution, was to spend $5 million a year on gliding instruction in "high schools, colleges, youth centers, and municipal parks." Said Congressman Melvin Maas of Minnesota: "I visualize the coming generation of Americans as a nation of boys and girls in gliders."

Others weren't so sure. Reported John Andrews, managing editor of *Air News* and *Air Tech*, in 1944: "Others see no place for gliders and gliding after the war because helicopters and conventional airplanes will be cheap, foolproof, and as common as the pre-war automobile."

Actually, for a few years not much happened at all in gliding, except that the old enthusiasts returning to the sport were joined by ex-Air Corps pilots who, though sick of power planes, nonetheless wanted to keep in touch with flying. Those first postwar glider contests, in fact, seemed more like reruns of assault training than anything else. In the 1946 national contest, of the 48 gliders entered, 38 of them were war surplus. In 1950, half the entries were still from the war. Even in 1960, 11 percent were leftover war gliders. And they didn't soar so well; their wings were stubby, their bodies chunky, and for a thermal to carry them aloft, it had to approach the intensity of a tornado. That the planes were able to compete at all is testimony to the ability of their pilots.

And those pilots were good. In 1956 only about 600 active glider pilots were sprinkled throughout the whole country—compared with tens of thousands in Europe. Yet in that year at the world championships held at St. Yan in eastern France, a United States soarer named Paul MacCready, Jr., flying a French Brequit 901, gathered 4,924 points, beating his nearest competitor by more than 1,000 points, to become the new world champion.*

Slowly, across the United States, gliders began to appear in quantity—over the beaches of the West Coast and the plains of Texas, above the Appalachian ridges, and across the ranges of the Sierra. The number of registered soaring enthusiasts passed the 1,000 mark in the mid-fifties, and by the early sixties had tripled that. Still, the United States lagged behind much of the rest of the Western world; in 1967 Germany had more than 900 clubs, while the whole North American continent had fewer than 200.

Today the United States seems to be catching up. But it has a long way to go. Sailplane production by Schweizer, the only truly solid American manufacturer, remains at about 100 a year. Says Paul Schweizer: "The country just won't

---

*In later years Paul MacReady gained worldwide fame as the designer of the Gossamer Albatross, the first pedal power aircraft to fly the English Channel, then, in 1981, as the builder of *Solar Challenger*, world's first plane to be powered by the sun.

support a larger production. One reason is that even after all this time, America is really just discovering gliding. We have, perhaps, 3,000 gliders; but in Germany, there are probably well over 10,000, even though the country is only about a third our size. And look at Switzerland: It has only 6 million people, but they own about 1,200 gliders. In the same proportion, America would have 400,000 gliders—nearly 135 *times* what we have."

One reason Europeans are so sailplane-conscious, Schweizer suggests, is that gasoline prices abroad have been so high that anyone who wanted to fly thought *first* of gliding—unlike potential pilots in the United States. But he foresees American gasoline prices eventually pushing power-plane rental out of reach. And with the increased use of inexpensive winch launching, more Americans will be looking toward sailplanes. Add to that the crossovers from hang gliding ("those enthusiasts will eventually get tired of wind in their faces, low performance, and the risks involved") and sailplane flying should finally enter that postwar boom everyone expected thirty-five years ago.

Chapter Four

Getting Started

Okay, let's say that you're interested in soaring, that you think you might like to take lessons, but you're not sure. The best thing to do, of course, is to take a ride—and doing so is surprisingly easy. The United States has about 150 glider schools or major clubs, and there's probably one within an easy drive of you. And for a relatively modest amount (typically $15 or $20), one of the instructors will be glad to take you up for a demonstration ride—particularly if he knows you're a potential sailplane pilot.

Probably the easiest way to find a school (if no close one is listed in the Appendix) is to call the local airport and ask for the operations office. Simply tell the manager that you're interested in taking glider lessons, and ask for his advice. If he can't help, look under "Government—United States," in your phone book's yellow pages, and under the subhead "Federal Aviation Administration," then ask anyone who answers.

When you locate a soaring facility, telephone to see if it's open all week. If so, and if your schedule permits, try to make your first visit on a weekday. Some gliderports are overwhelmed on weekends, while during the week there's plenty of time to spare—all the time you need to get your questions answered and to go for a ride with a pilot who can take his time.

Some people don't like that first ride. They'd rather have their feet on the ground. But such folks are rare; if you've gone to the trouble to find a field and to line up a ride, you'll probably be hooked halfway through that first flight. Back on the ground you'll climb out a little giddy, wondering how quickly you'll be able to solo—and probably worried about what it will cost. (Most likely not so much as you think.)

Chances are that your demonstration flight will be in a 600-pound Schweizer 2-33, since that is the most widely used trainer in the United States. (More than 500 have been built since 1967.) The first digit means it's a dual model, and the second means it's the 33rd design that Schweizer has produced. Compared with most sailplanes, with its high wing, angularity, and external struts, it's rather chunky, but it's solid, safe, dependable, and extraordinarily air-worthy. It has to be: students do some strange things in it.

It has dual controls, and you, the passenger, will be in the forward seat, while the pilot sits behind. You'll settle down into the comfortable, probably worn, contours of the seat with the control stick rising between your knees. The pilot will show you how to strap yourself in—a little tricky if you're not used to it. The instrument panel will stretch out before you, and you'll find that your feet come to rest on the rudder pedals. During the flight, the pilot won't mind if you keep them there, and if you lightly hold on to the stick to trace his control motions.

You'll be towed to 2,000 or 3,000 feet, and you'll soar for maybe twenty minutes. Probably the instructor will give you the controls for a brief try at simple maneuvers.

And when you land, your thoughts will center on the question Can I do it? The answer, with few exceptions: of course. If you've learned to drive a car, you can master a sailplane, and you'll do so a lot more quickly. For some the experience may be more fearful; after all, they point out, in an automobile one has the option of traveling at 15 mph, and of stopping on the shoulder if he is overcome by traffic. In a glider, though, the problems of traffic are relatively minor, there's no engine to worry about, and you don't even have to shift gears.

Consider what you are doing when you drive a 2,500-pound automobile at 55 mph along a country road: You're hoping that your aim of that missile will get you by other behemoths coming nearly at you, and you pass them within

4 or 5 feet at 110 mph—and you may do that all day long, utterly trusting your vehicle to behave as you expect it to, having faith that all those strangers driving all those other one-and-a-half-ton cars are rational, competent, and healthy, at least healthy enough not to pass out as they approach you.

Yes, you can learn to pilot a sailplane. The only requirements are that you be at least fourteen years old (sixteen to get your license). You can be ninety-five or more if you can still climb into that cockpit. You don't even have to be particularly healthy: The Federal Aviation Administration (which regulates all air-related activities in the United States) doesn't even require a physical examination for sailplane pilots. All an applicant must do to satisfy the bureaucracy is to sign a slip that says, "I certify that I have no known physical defect that makes me unable to pilot a glider."

When you do decide that you want to take lessons, hold off a bit; don't sign up with the next sailplane pilot who walks by. You are going to spend a lot of time with your instructor, so you should make sure that you get along well with him or her. Even more important, you want to find someone who is a *superb* teacher—someone who will be tough on you, who is a real professional, who is extraordinarily conscientious. He'll be laying the groundwork for the attitudes you'll hold for the rest of your life. Ask around before you sign up, and see what your potential teacher's reputation is. Then talk to him to get an estimate of total cost and what, in general, his lesson plan is. Ask questions; if he's too busy to talk to you in detail, he'll be too busy to spend the time necessary to teach. A poor or uninterested instructor won't only waste much of your time and money, but he may let you acquire habits that will prevent you from *ever* becoming a really superior soaring pilot.

Now that you've finally signed, and with the schedule roughly worked out with the instructor, here's a suggestion: Immediately join the Soaring Society of America (Suite 25, 3200 Airport Avenue, Santa Monica, CA 90405.)* A standard membership currently costs about $30, and it's a sound investment. You'll receive a large packet of material—lists and booklets and folders and directories, and even a sticker for your car window. Most important, you'll get a subscription to *Soaring*. Not only is the magazine crammed full of useful information, but the enthusiasm of the writers and the beauty of the illustrations are overwhelming—and this is vital for a beginning sailplane pilot. There will be times during your lessons when you will be really discouraged—when you make four rotten landings in a row, when you think you've finally got the aerotow technique put away and suddenly find yourself in the turbulent towplane wake (and

---

*See Appendix F for a list of comparable organizations in some seventy foreign countries.

Canopy of a two-place Lark so clean the pilot feels as though he's sitting in space. He's watching a student maneuver his Schweizer 2-33. (Dick Brown, State College, PA)

In 1980, Schweizer introduced its Sprint (SAC Model 1-36) "to fill the demand for an afford-able sailplane with Diamond Badge performance and good flying characteristics." It is ex-pected to take over from the 1-26, America's most popular sailplane. Maximum speed, 121 mph. Glide ratio, 31:1 at 53 mph. Minimum sink, 2.25 fps at 42 mph.   (Schweizer Aircraft)

The mark of a student pilot: He tries to keep himself upright rather than to relax and allow his body to align with the plane.

from behind you, from the instructor, only silence), when you start your takeoff with your canopy unlatched and hear your instructor gently mention that if left that way it will fly open. You will be discouraged. Actually, as you learn later, you're *expected* to make such mistakes; the coordination- and judgment-learning processes can be looked upon as a long series of small, corrected errors. Nevertheless, when you foul up you'll be depressed. And a prescription for that is to read the current issue of *Soaring*. You'll be so excited by it all that you'll overcome all those doubts; you'll just *have* to finish the course.

Soon your logbook (required by the FAA) will show an exciting story. It will tell about your first lesson, and those first tentative, uncoordinated, shallow turns. It will mention the turns, turns, turns of the next couple of flights, and then later of your practice at slow flight, and of the forward stalls you found yourself in. And it will note the first few very rough aerial tows—and then, eventually, they cease to be mentioned. If you are lucky, your instructor may note the time you accidentally caught a thermal and spiraled to 6,000 feet. That wasn't in the lesson plan, but he enjoyed it as much as you. Logged, too, will be the patterns, over and over, and those awful landings, and worse, the practice rope breaks, and then more landings and more landings, and you thought you'd never get them right and that you weren't getting any better at all and then . . .

Solo. You write this line in your logbook yourself, because *you* are the "pilot in command." And years later you'll look at that entry and remember how you felt at the time, how everyone always feels, no matter how cocky he has become: "Ohmygod; the instructor has lost his senses; he's making a terrible

Everyone's first log book tells its own dramatic story. (Rocky Miller)

Solo.

Solo. Yours truly gets initiated.

mistake. I'm not ready. Not *today*." And you'll remember how shocked you were when the towplane yanked the rope taut and the rear of the plane *slammed* down because your heavy copilot wasn't in there with you; *nobody* was back there to grab the controls, if. And you'll remember how, like a baby bird kicked out of his nest, you wanted that solo to be so *perfect*—and yet, because you don't get a second chance for a glider landing, your built-in conservativeness took over, so that you landed halfway up the field rather than chance setting down too early.

And you remember how silly you felt with the traditional grin spread across your face, a grin you tried to but couldn't remove, even when that half dozen people tromped across the field to congratulate you, and even when your instructor, brandishing scissors, cut out the sweaty back of your good L. L. Bean shirt in the traditional act that somehow nobody had ever informed you of.

Keep your logbook in nice shape. It contains a story worth telling.

SOLO—HOW LONG WILL IT TAKE?

Those who have never flown before should expect to fly two dozen times or more (including a few five-minute practice rope breaks) before solo. Some schools offer an accelerated course that can concentrate the lessons into a two-week vacation; but be prepared to work. An active power-craft pilot may need only a dozen glider flights in a "transition" course before he's ready to add the glider rating to his license.

Most instructors break the beginner's presolo process down into seven to ten lessons, each requiring at least one flight, and perhaps as many as five or more.

You can take lessons at a soaring school or you can join a club and pay for your training partly in work around the clubhouse, hangar, and field. In either case, the frequency of lessons is mostly up to you, although most instructors say that you probably shouldn't stretch the time between lessons to more than ten days or so.

You'll need a student license to solo, and you'll get that from an FAA examiner (perhaps your instructor). After solo, you've got two years to get your permanent license, or you'll have to renew. The big advantage in having a final license, of course, is that you can carry passengers.

To be eligible for a permanent license, a student must be knowledgable in meteorology, navigation, and Federal Aviation Regulations (the "FARs"), along with competence in the air, of course. He'll be soloing most of the time now (figure about fifty flights), and take a few additional dual flights with his instructor to learn such maneuvers as spins, to refine techniques and to break any bad habits that may be developing. Eventually, to prove it all to the FAA, he must take a not-so-easy written exam and a relatively easy flight test with an FAA examiner. And then he's a pilot.

If it sounds long and involved, think of the poor Soviet counterpart. He doesn't even get into the air until he's passed difficult tests in flight theory, meteorology, and navigation. Then during the first year of training, he learns how to bank. The second year, he masters aerotow. And if he's lucky, he gets to solo sometime in the third year.

But then, it *is* free.

Chapter Five

Why Gliders Glide

Flying a glider is a balancing act, a never-ending attempt to do three things: control speed, control direction, keep the plane streamlined. You control the speed with the elevators, the direction with the ailerons, the streamlining with the rudder. Just *how* gets a little more complicated. You control those three factors by balancing three elements: drag, lift, and gravity.

Haul your glider to the edge of a cliff, poke the nose over, get in, tip it forward, and note what happens. First—

Gravity begins to tug you downward. But does the glider plummet vertically, unencumbered? No. Not unless you are in a complete vacuum. (A leaf, too, in a vacuum would fall like a rock.) Instead, the ship encounters air, which immediately brings into action the second force—

43

Drag, the resistance to air. As the plane slides off the cliff, it pushes the air out of the way, and because the air doesn't move instantaneously, it slows the plane's drop. (Stick your hand out a car window and that's air-produced drag you feel.)

The plane, nose first, is diving, and its wings push through the air, parting it, so that some goes under the wing, some over, with the two streams recombining at the trailing edge. The wing is so designed that the upper surface is longer—from front to back—than the bottom, and the air traveling over the top becomes thinner than the air zipping underneath (more about that later). Through a combination of effects—

Lift is produced. The air supports the wings. The plane, meanwhile, in a slight nose-down attitude, more or less slides through the air, gliding downward, pulled by gravity. If the plane were pulled forward by a propeller, that force would be *thrust*. But in a glider, *gravity* does the work.

Your plane is sinking because of gravity, but it is being held up by lift; gravity is also pulling it forward, but not *too* fast, because of drag. Get a near-balance between those forces, and you have flight.

Meanwhile, you're losing altitude at the rate of, oh, 200 feet a minute.

However, a wind begins to strike the face of the cliff. It deflects upward at 260 feet a minute. Now, instead of losing altitude, you're rising at the gentle rate of 60 feet a minute. The nose still points downward, and you're still gliding *down* the air, but you and the air are rising as a unit.

That the air actually can blow up a hill was proven to me for the first time a decade ago during a climb up Maine's Mount Katahdin. We were on a two-foot ledge halfway up the north slope of Baxter Peak, a half mile or so above the valley floor, when thunderheads began to move in. Soon lightning was crashing around us, and we prepared to be drenched. We waited, expectant, but no torrent. It *seemed* to be raining, but we weren't getting wet. And then I eased forward and looked over the side, and got a face full of water. The rain was pouring *upward*, carried by the wind, while we stretched out in the lee of the ledge underneath us.

In the nineteen-twenties, Robert Kronfeld, one of Germany's more famous Wasserkuppe glider instructors, used to give his students this explanation of how a sailplane can rise: "Suppose you let a model glider fly down from the ceiling at one end of a room to the floor at the other end, and imagine a giant lifting the whole room high up into the air—then the model plane would be gaining in altitude while gliding downward." Soaring writer Richard Wolters uses the con-

cept of sailing a paper plane over a campfire. It glides downward until it encounters the rising column of hot air, then soars skyward.

Now, back to the wing again—back, in fact, to your arm still sticking out
of the car window. Hold your hand horizontal and you feel the pressure of the
air—the 55 mph relative airflow (or relative wind)—pushing it backward. (It's
called *relative* airflow, of course, because *it* isn't moving; *you* are, and it doesn't
matter which; what matters is only the wind relative to you.) Now tilt your hand's
front edge upward. You'll not be astonished to note that two things happen: First,
the backward tug, the *drag*, increases, mainly because you are exposing more
surface of your hand to that relative airflow. (You can't notice it, but that tiny
amount of extra drag has slightly slowed the speed of the car.)

The second thing you feel is that your hand, tilted upward, tends to rise.
This for two reasons: First, the air striking the bottom of your hand is more or less
beating it upward. More important, though, the air whizzing up and over your
hand is thinning a bit, causing a partial vacuum to develop on the topside, and
trying to suck your hand upward. The degree to which you have tilted your
hand, or, more properly, the angle at which the relative airflow meets your hand
(or a wing in flight), is called the *angle of attack*.

Probably everyone who is reading this has been told a dozen times how a
wing works. Here it is once again: Visualize the silhouette of a whale resting on
the ocean's surface—flat (or relatively so) on the bottom, bulged on top, particularly near the front end. That shape, exaggerated, is similar to the cross section of a wing, an *airfoil*.

Now imagine a wing with that cross section, moving, blunt end first,
through the air. The relative airflow separates at the leading edge, flows over the
wing's top and bottom to meet again at the trailing edge. Because the wing is
bulged across the top, the air, rising to go over it, thins. (You can think of the
plane in a wind tunnel, with the air moving across the top, going further, and
consequently thinning. That's not exactly right, but the result would be the
same.) As the air density drops, it exerts less pressure on the upper surface of
the wing, and generates lift.*

Now tilt the wing's front edge upward as it moves forward, increasing its
angle of attack. Air striking the lower surface is compressing, adding a hill of
pressure (called *dynamic* pressure) over which the wing must ride. And the air
flowing over the top will become even less dense (further reducing what's called
the *static* pressure), and the wing will tend even more to be sucked up into this
partial vacuum. As the angle of attack nears maximum lift angle, in fact, nearly

---

*The action is called the Bernoulli effect, which states that a fluid in motion exerts decreasing
pressure as its speed increases, an effect whose best-known application is a Venturi tube.

four fifths of the lift is coming from the decreased pressure on top, and not much more than one fifth is resulting from the dynamic pressure of that underwing mass of air hurling downward.* If the angle of attack becomes too great, of course, everything goes haywire. Severe eddies form behind the wing, relative airflow slams nearly head on into its upturned bottom, and overall lift decreases to impotence. A *stall* develops.

FOR EMPHASIS

Decrease the angle of attack and:
- Speed increases
- Lift decreases
- Drag decreases

Increase the angle of attack and:
- Speed decreases
- Lift increases
- Drag increases

The primary control surfaces of a sailplane number three. The *elevator*, by affecting the plane's pitch, controls the wing's angle of attack, and like a bicyclist rolling down a hill and changing the hill's slope angle, ultimately determines speed. The *ailerons* cause the plane to roll, and as a result the wings more or less lift it around, changing the direction of flight. And the *rudder* helps out by keeping everything streamlined and efficient.

In more detail:

The Ailerons, movable flaps on the trailing edge of the wings, are controlled by the stick. Because they work opposite each other (when one goes up, the other goes down), they cause the plane to roll, to control the bank angle. That angle determines the rate of turn: the steeper the bank, of course, the quicker the turn.

The Elevator's primary function is to change the wing's angle of attack, and as a consequence alters potential lift, drag, and speed. Push the stick forward and the elevator points downward, causing the tail, in response, to rise, while the front of the plane tilts downward, and the craft begins to gather speed. To slow it again, the pilot pulls back on the stick, causing the elevator to point

---

*Actually, the lift pressure required is quite small. If the glider weighs 600 pounds and has a wing area of 150 square feet, that means that each square inch of wing need support only 2 1/4 ounces. (150 x 144 sq. in. = 21600/9600 oz. = 2.25)

upward. As the plane's nose begins to shift upward, the wing's angle of attack increases, and the craft slows.

The Rudder, surprisingly, does *not* make the aircraft turn. If you hold the plane level and stomp down on one of the rudder pedals, the plane will swivel so that it is *pointed* in a somewhat different direction, but the direction of travel doesn't change. You just skid along sideways. What does the rudder do, then? It guards against what is called *aileron drag* or adverse yaw.

Parts of a sailplane, with few exceptions, are nearly identical with those of a powercraft. The most obvious difference (other than the wing, disproportionately long for the body) is the wheels—usually one near the front (with a skid protecting the nose), another in back, and perhaps a small wheel or skid mounted on fist-size springs at the tip of each wing.

The standard design for the tail assembly (also called *empennage*) on a high-performance sailplane is as shown, but some designs employ only a large V, which acts as a combined stabilizer-elevator-rudder system. Standard style usually has the horizontal stabilizer-elevator unit resting near the bottom of the fin.

One item not found on a power plane is a set of *spoilers* or *dive brakes*. Spoilers are yard-long plates atop the wing that rise to "spoil" airflow and lift, allowing the pilot to get down quickly. Dive brakes, usually longer, emerge from both top and bottom of wings.

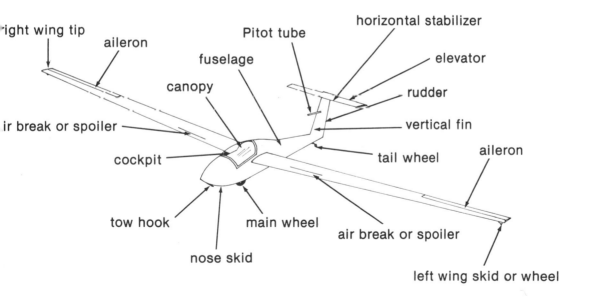

Sailplane nomenclature.

Cabin floor in a 2-33 with rudder pedals and compartment for ballast, used if pilot weighs below a specified amount or if rearseat passenger is heavy. Control stick is in foreground.

To understand, take another look at what is happening as you use the ailerons to bank. Shove the stick to the left and the right aileron goes down. It effectively changes the shape of the wing's airfoil, so that it increases the angle of attack and produces more lift, and the wing rises. Over on the left, meanwhile, the aileron flips to point upward, and down goes that wing. Now the plane is ready to bank around the circle.

But there's a problem. Not only does that high wing have more lift, but because the angle of attack has increased, it also has a little extra drag, enough so that the plane's nose tends to yaw to the right, opposite to the left turn. You'll get around eventually, but the turn won't be clean; the plane will be going a little sideways. Any sloppy, uncoordinated turn produces excess drag and subsequent loss of altitude.

The rudder, thanks to Wilbur Wright, is there ready to compensate for that aileron drag. It yaws the nose around in the direction of the turn, and the relative airflow can then sweep along the body without excess drag. That's flying clean.

When you fly clean, you know it because of an almost indispensable instrument (also invented by Wilbur Wright) that has the distinction of being the least expensive part of the sailplane. It's the yaw string, a 2- or 3-inch hunk of yarn taped to the center of the canopy or maybe to the *pitot* tube (a soda straw-

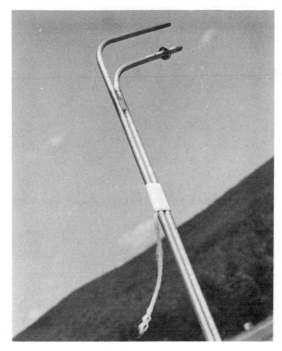

Pitot and static tubes. Pitot has its front end open into the wind to measure impact (ram) pressure, while the static tube, with holes or slits in the sides, measures static air pressure. The combination drives such instruments as altimeter, variometer, and airspeed indicator. Dangling from it is the yaw string, a snip of yarn secured by tape.

size aluminum tube pointing forward to measure air pressure). It's right there in front where you can keep your eye on it. Your job is to keep it straight, because a straight yaw string means that the aircraft is streamlined—that no significant relative airflow is blowing the yaw string to one side or another—which in turn means that the fuselage is not moving sideways through the air. The yaw string is an arrow pointing to the rudder pedal that should be pushed.

If, during a turn, you keep the string centered, and if you hold the nose so that it seems to skim the horizon (in most trainers), you have what's called a *coordinated* turn. "Sweep the horizon with your paintbrush," my instructor used to say. Never did make much sense, but somehow it helped. When it didn't, "Don't be impulsive," he'd say impulsively. "Make it smooth, like a ballet! A ballet!" I'd try to. Then sometimes—usually, as I remember, during landing-approach turns, when I didn't want to hear *anything*—his voice would become very calm. "You *will* keep that yaw string straight," he'd say, and I knew that he meant it.

When a glider—controls coordinated and banked correctly—enters a moderate turn, the pilot can largely straighten the rudder and level the ailerons, and the plane will continue to turn. Just as in straight and level flight, it feels *stable*. In calm weather, if you take your hands and feet from the controls, for a while the plane will tend to carry on as though it were on auto pilot.

Why Gliders Glide 49

Sailplanes have relatively few instruments to monitor. Airspeed indicator, driven by the pitot tube, shows indicated airspeed—here in mph, but in European ships in kmph. Redline ("never exceed" line) speed is painted directly on the dial; here (difficult to see in black and white) it rests at 98 mph.

Altimeter must be set before each flight. (Here, it hasn't been; indicates an altitude of 745 feet.) After landing pattern is begun, instructor in this training glider can flip white cut-out over instrument face. The large hand indicates hundreds of feet, the middle-size hand, thousands, and the small hand (here, pointing virtually straight up) ten thousands. Figures in window at instrument's right indicate the barometric pressure.

Vane-type variometer operates like a power plane's rate-of-climb indicator, but quicker, with more sensitivity. Some variometers consist of two tubes containing a red and a green pith ball separated by a scale. When the green ball rises, so does the glider; when the red ball rises, the glider is sinking. Other variometers are equipped with tones that change in pitch or "clicks" that increase in frequency to indicate rates of climb, enabling a pilot to concentrate his attention outside the cockpit. For serious cross-country flying, variometers are also equipped with MacCready (or "speed-to-fly") rings, which, based on rate-of-climb rates within thermals, indicate the speed to fly between thermals for best cross-country speed.

Air vent is used not only during summer to cool off the cockpit, but in winter to drive frost buildup from the canopy. Other instruments often found: slip or skid indicator, gyro-driven attitude indicator, magnetic compass, outside air-temperature gauge, accelerometer or G-meter, radio equipment.

In a sense, it is, because of its built-in stability, what British pilot-writer Derek Piggot calls "the balancing act." Sailplanes (and power planes as well) are designed as much as possible to fly without the help of the pilot.

To understand the forces at work, start with the plane's center of gravity. When an aircraft rolls, it does so around a line that passes through the nose and out the tail. Visualize a rod stuck through a model plane. If correctly placed, when the rod is held horizontally, the plane will stay put even if upside down or on its side.

Now pull out the rod and insert it again from top to bottom, through the line around which the plane yaws. Extract it and stick it this time through the side, through the pitch axis. The three holes intersect at the center of gravity, and for the balancing act to be effective, the plane must be stable in those three areas: yaw, roll, and pitch.

• *Yaw stability* is the easiest to understand. The rear part of a sailplane is long, narrow, and relatively light; the front is bulbous, heavy (it contains, among other objects, you), and short. The balance point is obviously somewhere close to the front end. Without the wings, in fact, the craft looks something like a bloated arrow, or a weathervane, and that's one reason it's stable. If for some reason—a sharp gust of wind, for example—the plane starts sliding even slightly sideways, it immediately tends to *weathervane* into the relative airflow. It quickly becomes stable.

• *Roll stability* is ensured by aircraft designers through the use of *dihedral*. Look at a plane from the front and you'll notice that the wings attach to the body at a slight angle, like a very flat V. Now, still looking from the front, visualize the plane blown into a bank by an eddy of wind. The wings are pulling up at an angle now, and because there's not so much lift, the plane starts to drop. As it descends, the wing that is low presents a broad face to the upward-flowing air, while the other wing, pointing somewhat upward, does not. The airflow forces the low wing up, and roll stability results.

• *Pitch stability* is a little more complex, but it's very clever. Look again at that balance-point hole that you punched through the side of your model, and you may be surprised to see that it is in *front* of the wing (or at least in front of the point of maximum lift of the wing, called the *center of pressure*). If the wing were the only surface involved, you'd never get off the ground; as soon as you would become airborne, the wing would lift you, swinging around the balance point, right back to the runway again. You'd hop down the field like a jackrabbit.

To overcome this rotational force, designers attach the stabilizer at a somewhat different angle from that of the wing. Often you can't tell, but on most sailplanes the wings seem to be mounted onto the body with a slight upward tilt (called the *angle of incidence*) of their leading edge. But the horizontal stabilizer seems to be mounted level or even pointing downward. It produces a slight downward load, so that it tends to push the tail down just enough to offset the forces that are pushing down the nose. So you have the tail and nose pressing downward while the wings pull up, and like a three-legged stool, all is in balance, stable.

In level flight all the forces work beautifully together so that you haven't much more to do than take in the scenery. But during turns, a few curlicues pop up that at first seem to invalidate all those lovely stability principles.

In a shallow turn, because the dihedral tends to tug the lower wing back upward, you must maintain a touch of aileron, just enough to offset the tendency for the plane to level itself. In a steep turn, however, you have the opposite problem—something called *overbanking tendency*. In a high angle of bank, the plane's outboard wing is traveling significantly faster than the inboard wing, so it has more lift. The pilot, then, must apply opposite aileron, against the turn, to keep the turn coordinated.

The idea of an overbanking tendency, by the way, disturbs many students. They fear that if they bank too far, the plane will somehow flip over. It won't. As soon as it nears an angle of bank anywhere close to vertical, it will slide down sideways and right itself. And no plane can fly at a 90-degree angle of bank. There's nothing to hold it up.

During a turn you have to compensate for that weathervane effect, too. Because the aircraft is straight instead of curved, when it is in a turn the tail actually is sticking out of the side of the turning circle. (Think of a 100-foot plane turning in a 50-foot circle and it becomes easier to visualize.) The weathervaning tries to straighten the flight path, so the pilot must maintain a small amount of rudder simply to keep going smoothly around the circle.

And there's one more effect to think about. Because the plane is in a roll position, the wings don't produce as much vertical lift as they do in horizontal flight. The tendency, then, is to slip downward. So to compensate, to hold your altitude instead of doing a slow spiral downward, you must increase the wing's angle of attack, must maintain a relative nose-high attitude. You do so, of course, by holding back on the stick.

This all sounds complex, and in detail, it is. But the fact is, as soon as you experience various turns, you come to sense what is needed, and with practice you automatically adjust. So why should you know the theory? So that when you're learning you're not upset if the plane reacts unexpectedly, and so that you don't think something is wrong with you or the plane.

That sixth sense of realizing quickly when something is wrong *does* develop, and it becomes quite reliable. Even a beginning pilot will, for instance, recognize when his plane is about to go into a stall. And an experienced pilot is continually listening to his craft, feeling what it is saying to him. A *power* pilot is guided by needles pointing at numbers. His training, in fact, includes flying for a short time with a hood over his head to stop him from looking outside. But a glider pilot's attention is outside the cockpit almost all the time. Head on a swivel, he's watching the horizon, the sky, the ground, and every so often, of course, his instruments. But he need only scan them; he sweeps his eyes across them, taking a second or two, then he's searching the sky again.

One common mistake of beginners is that, particularly in turns, they attempt to achieve accurate, smooth sweeps by watching their airspeed indicator. They've learned, you see, that a high airspeed means not enough back pressure on the stick; that the nose was allowed to drop. Slow airspeed, on the other hand, means that a stall might be imminent, and no beginning flyer wants *that*. The problem is that the amateur "chases the airspeed," a habit that results in porpoising.

Closely related is *overcontrolling*—using too much control, then having to pull back in the opposite direction—one of the most common errors of the beginner. A novice should try to think in terms of stick *pressures* rather than movements. And both stick and pedals should be handled with firm friendship, not stomped and throttled. Relax your feet on the pedals and you might discover that the tenseness was causing you to press with unequal pressure. You might also find that you'll begin to detect other things the rudder is trying to tell you. I can remember one time early in my lessons when I happened to glance at my right hand, and found it mottled white from holding the stick as though it were a cobra's neck. I relaxed my hand, and my whole body seemed to sigh.

Some beginners, however, have the opposite problem, the same problem that some people have who are learning to ride horseback. Gliders are so easy to fly that some new pilots relinquish responsibility to the plane. You must be firm; crosswind landings and tows through turbulence and emergency maneuvers require a firm, no-back-talk attitude, even though you must continue to sense what's happening.

This sense of what your plane is doing is most easily dramatized by the stall. What happens in a stall is that the airfoil reaches and exceeds what's called the *critical angle of attack*. That means that the relative airflow passing over the wing begins to tear away from the surface, until it no longer is sufficient to hold the plane up.

A good deal of consideration should be given to stalls, because unlike power planes, gliders often fly at airspeeds relatively close to the stall speed, and turbulence (or just plain sloppy flying) can much more easily lead to a stall.

Let's say that you're trying to stay up in a very weak thermal, and you get so wrapped up in feeling for it that you ignore the warning signs of an upcoming stall and suddenly find yourself in one. What has happened is that you pulled the stick back farther and farther, trying somehow to *climb*. The air that was flowing over the top of the airfoil simply couldn't make that increased bend, and instead

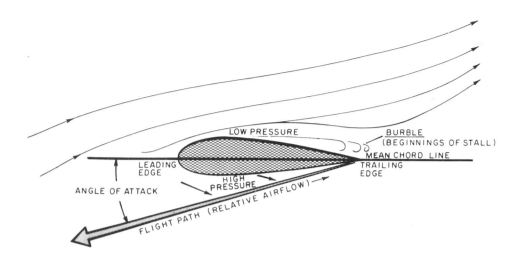

An airfoil, and the forces acting upon it.

---

of flowing smoothly over the wing top, it began to break away at what's called the *separation point*. And as it did so it no longer produced lift.

This breakaway begins at the trailing edge of the inboard wing section and works its way forward and outward. Designers planned it that way, twisting the wing slightly so that the angle of attack is greater near the plane's body. Even when the inboard section has ceased being useful in developing lift, the outboard section is still functioning. That's where the ailerons are, and the builder wants you to be able to use those as long as possible.

A conventional, low-speed stall usually begins to make itself known in obvious ways:

Low airspeed. A pilot is a little low in a pattern, for example, and subconsciously pulls back on the stick, farther and farther, in an attempt to hold his aircraft up, and his speed gets lower and lower and . . . .

Mushy controls. At high airspeeds, the controls seem heavy, stiff, resisting. At low airspeed (under 40 mph or so in most trainers), control pressure is lighter, more easily applied. Close to a stall it becomes sloppy and mushy.

Nose-high attitude. If you wonder where the horizon went, that might mean you're nearing a stall. Get that nose down.

Silence. What's that? you ask, and cock your ear. It's the sound of silence, the sound of no wind whistling past the canopy, the sound of impending stall.

Sometimes, too, there's a little shudder of the aircraft or a little pulsing or buffet in the stick just before the plane pitches forward. Often it's too subtle to notice, and your attention has just been caught by the horizon suddenly flashing up over the canopy.

The stall speed of a given plane isn't *always* the same. Weight has a lot to do with the variation (a passenger will raise the stall speed), and so does the center of gravity—changed by that same passenger. Turns raise the stall speed considerably. A 60-degree angle of bank, for instance, effectively doubles the weight of the aircraft, and that increases the stall speed by 40 percent. So if your Schweizer 2-33 trainer ordinarily stalls at 32 mph, do a 60-degree bank and your stall speed has risen to nearly 45 mph. (Remember: "A 60-degree angle of bank increases the stall speed by 40 percent." It's on nearly every FAA test.)

Other things that effect stall speed: dive brakes or spoilers, gusts or turbulence, generally sloppy flying, and material on the surface of the plane—dirt, dents, ice, frost, even bugs. (Take a high-performance sailplane up late on a hot, muggy summer afternoon and by the time you come down, the plane won't fly so well anymore, simply because of the number of splattered bugs.)

Recovery from simple stalls becomes nonchalant. Let the plane do the work. Move the stick forward a bit. *Just* a bit. Wait a moment. Return to normal flight. The mistake that many students make is to overreact; they push the stick too far forward. If you feel yourself lift from your seat, that isn't a stall, it's negative Gs, and it probably happened because you pushed the stick forward before the stall was actually in effect. How far forward you should push the stick depends on such factors as kind of plane and how deeply you're stalled, but in no case do you slam it forward and hold it there. Most times (particularly in trainers) a simple relaxation of back pressure is enough. Usually the whole thing is so gentle your unsuspecting aunt riding along wouldn't even notice.

Another fault with beginners is a tendency upon recovery to bring the nose back up too high again and stall the second time. That secondary stall doesn't matter much when you're experimenting with stalls high in the air, or even if you're chasing a thermal and stall out and lose it. It matters a lot, however, if you double-stall in a high-stress situation—in your landing pattern, for instance.

How might it happen? You're just beginning your pattern, perhaps, when you suddenly realize that you hadn't noticed a high-performance plane that was already in *his* pattern (larger than yours because of his lower glide ratio), and so you make the first of a series of wrong decisions: You decide to do a 360-degree turn to use up some time.

You complete the circle with a great deal of embarrassment, because halfway through you realize that you've made a mistake. (Below 1,000 feet you should never turn away from the airport.) And you're sure that your instructor is down there on the field watching. So you're thinking more about that than about your pattern, and suddenly realize that you're getting low. That's too bad, because after that dumb maneuver, the least you could do would be to land in the right place instead of way down near the beginning of the field.

So without thinking you automatically pull back on the stick to stretch your glide, and so preoccupied are you that you miss all those danger signs yelling at you through your senses; you don't hear the silence, you don't see the horizon move down, you don't feel the controls mush.

And then you stall. As you suddenly see in great detail the ground and the hangar and the upturned faces, you say to yourself, "My God; I'm *stalling*, and everyone is watching, and I look really stupid, and it isn't even my plane," and you quickly recover. But in your excitement and panic and confusion, you pull the nose up again, and then "burrrr," there's that little shudder that means another stall—and statistically this one, the secondary stall, is the one that leads to crumpled planes and pilots.

That's particularly so if the stall is during the turn, where, unfortunately, it usually is. Recovery from turning stalls is considerably more difficult than from straight-and-level stalls—mainly because you have to overcome your natural reactions. If, in a straight-ahead stall one wing drops (because, perhaps, a gust touched it just as you began the stall), you automatically tend to try to pick up the dropping wing with the ailerons. But you'll find that it does no good to try, because the turbulence of the air around the trailing edge of that downed wing makes the aileron useless. Trying to pick up the low wing with ailerons, in fact, simply makes things worse.

To straighten yourself up again, use opposite rudder as you ease the stick forward. The rudder will swing that downed wing forward, and even that little extra speed will smooth the air out so that the wing will begin to right itself; *then* apply a little aileron, if necessary.

One wing dropping during the beginning of a stall is also called an *incipient spin*, because it's looked upon as a spin's first stage. (To guard against your blood pressure rising, your instructor might call it "cross-control stall" when he tells you what will be the lesson of the day.) But a conventional glider will never go into a spin unless the pilot either wants it to spin (and even then maybe it won't) or he grossly misuses the controls. To enter a spin in most trainers, as one wing is stalled, the glider is widely yawed with the stick held in the aft position until after perhaps a full turn in a slow spiral.* Finally, the plane will enter a rapid spin, and if nothing is done, it might continue corkscrewing right into the earth.

Recovery from the first stage is easy: opposite rudder, stick moved slightly forward. In a full spin, the method is slightly different and should be learned, even though the information may never be used. If, somehow, you get into that

---

*In some planes, however, you apply only rudder, in others, only ailerons, in still others, both. Check your manual or instructor.

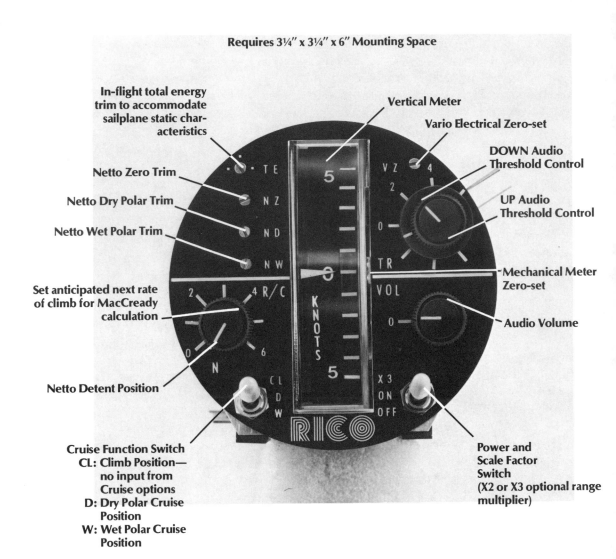

In-flight total energy trim to accommodate sailplane static characteristics

Netto Zero Trim

Netto Dry Polar Trim

Netto Wet Polar Trim

Set anticipated next rate of climb for MacCready calculation

Netto Detent Position

Cruise Function Switch
CL: Climb Position—
no input from
Cruise options
D: Dry Polar Cruise
Position
W: Wet Polar Cruise
Position

Vertical Meter

Vario Electrical Zero-set

DOWN Audio
Threshold Control

UP Audio
Threshold Control

Mechanical Meter
Zero-set

Audio Volume

Power and
Scale Factor
Switch
(X2 or X3 optional range
multiplier)

When a sailplane is abruptly dived or pulled up, a standard variometer may incorrectly indicate a high rate of lift. This is called a "stick thermal," and it can add a touch of confusion. A "total energy system" eliminates the problem. Most such instruments include a small Venturi in the air stream; when connected to the static outlet of the variometer it tends to cancel out dive- and climb-caused errors. A further development is the Netto. It also cancels out the craft's sink rate (at whatever speed it is flying), and gives a reading of the vertical movement of the surrounding air mass, regardless of whether the glider is descending or rising. Shown above is a combination of everything, a Rico Model VACS, which includes a gust damper, an audio signal (with automatic volume boost at high speeds), up-and-down threshold control, Netto, total-energy compensator, and electronic, zero-reading MacCready indicator. (Redwood Instrument Co., Redwood City, CA) position, you'll have little time to look up the steps. As advocated by the FAA:

1. Full opposite rudder.
2. After rotation slows, apply brisk, positive, straightforward movement of elevator control. (Do not be slow and cautious.)
3. Pause until rotation stops.
4. Centralize all controls, then level off.*

You should memorize this because of step 2. Looking straight at the ground and traveling at what seems to be an incredible speed, you won't feel much like pushing the stick forward. But don't worry; your instructor will guide you through a spin or two, and even if you never use the knowledge, knowing that you *can* will give you confidence.

In stopping a spin, in all of the control movements in flying, in fact—throughout the whole range of maneuvers—a novice should think like the Zen archer who believes he is part of his bow, and who *wills* the arrow to the target. My old karate teacher used to tell me that I was a leaf filling with rain that when full would tip and empty. I never understood him (and used to get kicked trying to figure it out)—and only now that I soar in a sailplane can I really understand what he meant.

---

*For your particular plane, check the owner's manual.

Chapter Six

Getting Up

In the good old days, to launch your glider all you needed were friends. *Strong* friends. Early Wright gliders were launched as the pilot lay prone, while two comrades—one on each wing tip—picked up craft and pilot and ran with them down a slope, into the wind. This method, fortunately, gave way to the use of shock cord, a rubber rope designed to give spring to landing gears. Here you needed *many* friends—a dozen or more. While four or five of them would sit on the ground at the brow of a hill, holding back the plane, the rest would stretch the shock cord into a giant slingshot, pulling the two ends until the pressure rose so high the holders couldn't hang on. They'd let go, and the plane suddenly would zip forward, catapulting from the hill. Simple, efficient, and cheap.

But it didn't get you very high. And there were minor problems, too. Here is a quote from a 1929 *National Geographic* explaining the procedures:

As the glider snaps into the air, men pulling the starter-rope duck to each side to escape possible injury should the take-off be clumsy . . . . Starts that go straight up into the air may look very racy, but are extremely dangerous, because the plane is liable to slip backward.

Today, even though some sailplanes are launched by means of automobiles and winches (see *Autotow and Winching*), the airplane tow, at least in the United States, has become standard. It's relatively expensive, but safe, effective, and, after a half dozen tows, easy. And whereas an auto or winch can fling you to maybe a thousand feet,* a plane can take you to any height and drop you into a thermal as well.

The takeoff sequence, of course, involves more than just the method of getting the plane into the air. It begins, in fact, with the *preflight*, the flyer's inspection of the plane—a routine that every pilot, almost by definition, takes seriously. As "pilot in command," he is not only responsible, but like a ship's captain he is boss. Beginning pilots have a difficult time learning this—learning that they are *not* to be rushed by impatient tow pilots, that checking each critical bolt on the aircraft is not petty, that a refusal to accept a frayed towrope is respected.

The preflight consists of two phases: An overall inspection before the plane is rolled onto the field, and the cockpit check just before takeoff. In the overall preflight, you check for three things:

1. *Airworthiness*. Is the aircraft in reasonable mechanical condition? Has it been properly cared for? Has all ripped fabric been patched? Do the parts move easily, as though properly oiled and greased? Is the tire inflated, the canopy clean, the paint presentable?

2. *Damage*. If you're using a club or instruction glider, lord only knows what the last pilot did to it. He may have landed so hard something sprung. He may improperly have tried aerobatics. He may have left the canopy open to be blown closed, breaking off the latch, which could allow it to blow open during the tow.

3. *Assembly*. Is the plane put together properly? If the last pilot made an off-field landing, the wings may have been removed for towing, then bolted on again incorrectly. Or the ailerons may have been connected backward. That's something you want to discover on the ground rather than 500 feet up.

To get the craft out on the field, ready for tow, you have to push or pull it, and this procedure itself takes some instruction. You *can* move it by yourself by pulling on the nose handle or on alternate wing struts or at built-in handholes or at the reinforced edge of the cockpit (depending on the model). But usually

---

*In the nineteen-thirties, a Toledo, Ohio, club was autolaunching gliders in winter to 3,000 feet by pulling them on the frozen Maumee River with 5,000-foot towlines of piano wire.

Preflight often begins with an examination of the open pitot tube—a favorite hiding place for spiders.

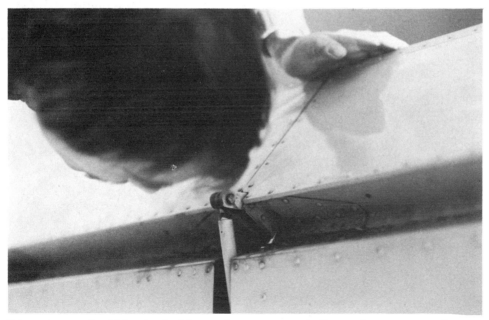

Aileron hinges should be checked for cracks, rust, ice, overall smooth operation, and proper tightness.

If the previous pilot abruptly yanked out full dive breaks while the plane was at excessive speed, the plates could have bent and now may bind.

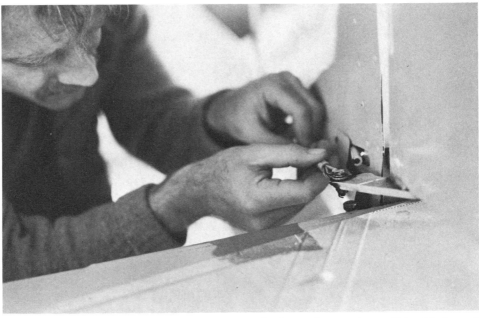

Pilot checks the nut where a rudder cable is attached to make sure that nothing binds, and that the nut isn't working loose.

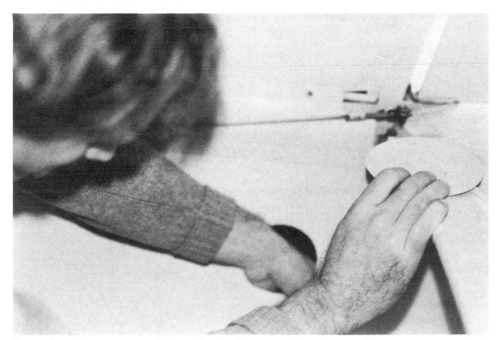

Some planes have pop-out disks in the fuselage near the tail, a good inspection port to look inside for ice accumulation in winter, porcupines in summer.

If wing-tip wheel inspection reveals damage, closely check the wing itself. The previous pilot could have whacked the ground upon landing.

Preflight includes cleaning the canopy, here practiced by Karl Striedieck. Polaroid glasses help reduce any remaining glare.

Detachable rear wheel, held in place by leather girdle, is lifted by handle on some high-performance sailplanes. It's removed for takeoffs and landings.

One way to move a plane is to pull and push on the cowling. Another is to haul it with a short rope hooked to the tow hook. (Rocky Miller)

An easier way to move a 1-26. Stay close to the fuselage. (Rocky Miller)

there's someone around to help you. Better watch him, though, to see that he doesn't push on a critical spot. If he shoves on the wing's trailing edge, for instance, he could bend it.

Push-pull-lift areas vary from model to model, but usually it's safe to apply pressure on struts, tips, and leading edges of wings, on the tail assembly's leading edges near the fuselage, and, with the canopy thrown open, on the structural section around the cockpit. Many models lend themselves best to the tail-first technique: Two people lift the forward edge of the horizontal stabilizer close to the fuselage and, facing aft, push the plane backward.

Easier than pushing by hand is to use a tow vehicle. (Ride-around lawn-mowers seem to be gaining favor.) An old aerotow line, at least the length of the sailplane's wingspan, is ideal. One danger here is that when the pulling vehicle stops rolling, the sailplane may not. Another is that when the plane is being hauled by car, the driver may tighten the rope so swiftly the sailplane catapults into the auto's rear. To guard against these possibilities, open dive brakes, tow slowly, and use a person at each wing tip.

Out on the field, finally, seated in the plane, the pilot goes through his cockpit preflight—and for this he has the help of an acronym. At least half a dozen of them are about, but probably the most widely used is:

CB SIT CB

Controls. Check them—everything that can be thought of as a control. Move the stick forward and back, then from side to side. Does it feel right, neither loose nor stiff? Do the ailerons move in the right direction? (First think about what they *should* do, then look to see if they do. Someone could have reversed the control rods during the last assembly.) Check the release knob to see that it has tension and slides smoothly. Adjust the trim and open the dive brakes or spoilers to see that they feel normal. Is your seat adjusted; can you move all controls their full range without stretching or cramping yourself? Rudder pedals feel okay? Pay particular attention to their cables to make sure the last person, shorter or taller than you, didn't leave them out of your adjustment. One champion pilot tells of the time during a tow that her rudder cables snapped out of position, jumping to the slot designed to accommodate a six-foot-plus pilot, which she is not. She had to slide down in her seat so far that when she landed the sailplane looked pilotless.

Ballast. In your overall preflight (before you got in), you should have looked under your cushion to see that the previous rider didn't leave his set of scuba weights that he uses as ballast. Now you check again between the rudder pedals (if that's the appropriate place in your plane) to see that no weight has been left there—unless you need it, of course. Check also to make sure that your

High-performance sailplanes gain a little more efficiency when junctions are taped—especially on wing and tail surfaces.

Tight shoulder straps will keep this pilot from hitting her head on the canopy if she encounters turbulence.

weight and that of your passenger conforms to the center-of-gravity placement, that the ratio of passenger-to-pilot weight is within the placard limitations. (By the way, make sure that you *understand* it. Some manufacturers—Schweizer, for example—continue to use formulas that to many pilots remain baffling.)

Straps. Are they comfortably snug? Tight enough so that in turbulence you'll feel as though you are really a part of the aircraft? Has your passenger figured out how to put his on?

Instruments. Turn on everything you should. Set the altimeter and check the other instruments to see if they're reading correctly. Does your variometer indicator show that you are sinking? Does your airspeed reading show you to be in reverse? Remember the errors so you won't be surprised later.

Trim. Put handle in normal takeoff position. Make sure it's secure.

Canopy. You'll probably remember to close it. You may not remember to lock it (or the canopy in back). That may be disastrous, because it could blow open during the tow. (If it does open, don't try to close it until you get off tow. Then, at a slower speed, relatively composed, you may be able to secure it. If not, and if it interferes with your flying, jettison it.) Some beginning pilots have been killed when their canopy blew open. They panicked, tried to close it, and lost control of the aircraft.

Brakes. Close the dive brakes (thus releasing your wheel brake) and *lock the handle in position*—a step often forgotten by beginning pilots. If the brakes aren't locked, during tow they can slowly suck open, and the towplane probably can't pull a glider with its dive brakes extended.

Most pilots eventually augment the standard cockpit check to reflect their own plane, or their own forgetfulness. Karl Striedieck, who holds the world's out-and-return distance record (1,016 miles), says that one problem with glider flying is the irregularity of it all. "Various locations, different crewpersons, different ships, to say nothing of distractions and pre-takeoff hassles, all provide fertile ground for omission of an important, if not hazardous, step in rigging and flight preparation," he once wrote in *Soaring*. "The obvious solution is a checklist." His:

Controls checked
Speed brakes checked, locked
Gear locked
Water connected
Radio checked
Altimeter set
MPC (maps, photos, calculator) in place
Tail wheel off
Barograph on

He also admits that he won't trust to memory the landing gear-lowering ceremony, that he must have help to remember. His reminder is a spring clamp on the spoiler handle that is removed only after the landing gear is lowered.

Sometime during your cockpit check, the wing runner will connect the towline—usually a 150-foot, quarter-inch rope of polypropylene. (Back when it was nylon the pilot felt like he was at the end of a rubber band.) Hookup won't happen until after you're strapped in, for to do so before is taboo. In fact, if you decide to leave the sailplane to go to the bathroom, you must pull the release knob first—a custom that guards against towplanes hauling aloft pilotless gliders. The towline-connection procedure goes like this:

1. "Open," says the wingman, and you pull the release knob.
2. "Close," he says, and you let it slide back forward.
3. "Test," says he, and pulls the line. You pull the knob and he jerks back, catching his balance.
4. "Open; close," the wingman says as the line is attached once again.

When sailplane pilot pulls towline release knob, trigger at left moves left, allowing finger-shaped ring holder to swing down and to the right.

As part of the preflight, the pilot should test the release mechanism as the wing runner pulls on the tow rope. (Rocky Miller)

Towline connected, return to the cockpit check. Pros remember where they left off; novices forget. Now the wingman walks toward the tip and signals the towplane (by swinging his arm) to take up slack. The towplane eases forward until the line is tight. The wingman now waits for you to tell him you're ready, that your cockpit check is complete. You give a thumbs-up sign, and he lifts the wing that was resting on the ground. "To me, this is always the beginning of life to a flight," Robert N. Buck, former TWA senior captain, once said. "The sailplane no longer lies on its side, inanimate and lifeless; now it seems to have awakened."

You signal by lustily waggling your rudder. The tow pilot will probably see that; he'll certainly see the wingman, who, in response to you, is whirling his arm around, a secondary signal for the towplane to start the flight.

Suddenly the sailplane jerks forward, nose lifting (because the tow ring is low), lurching ungainly as the wing runner keeps the plane level. But he need run only 10 feet or so. That's far enough; the air flowing over the wings steadies the plane, and you're on your own. You may note—on high-performance planes especially—a tendency for the right wing to bound downward when the runner releases. That's caused by the prop wash of the towplane. Anticipate it and you'll have no trouble.

If you have no wing runner, you start with one wing resting on the ground, then throw on full aileron to get that wing up as the plane starts to roll. If during the takeoff roll you feel that you are tail-heavy, that your rear is dragging, push the stick just a touch forward, and if the nose skid begins to rub, ease back a little. You probably won't have to do either.

The takeoff itself will happen without your help when the sailplane reaches 30 mph or so. The problem is not in getting off, but in holding the plane down. Try to keep the sailplane within a few feet of the ground by applying forward pressure on the stick. You're traveling at 60 or 65 mph now, and the sailplane is balanced to fly at 40 or so, so it has a tendency to rise. If you let it, the towplane won't be able to get off the ground.

AUTOTOW AND WINCHING

Today in the United States few gliders are launched by winch or autotow. But because of the skyrocketing price of fuel, that will probably change—particularly where runways are atop mountains, or in ridge-soaring areas where the launch site is adjacent to the hill.

If you're used to aerotow, the first time you're launched by auto or winch will be—well, memorable, because suddenly you're not in an aircraft anymore, but in a kite, climbing at an angle that is frighteningly steep. You don't really "fly" the plane up there; you more or less ride along, controlling your missile as it is projected into space.

Until you're airborne, the procedure is identical to aerotow. After leaving the ground, you fly level for a bit, then apply pressure to gently climb to 100 feet or so, also pretty much like aerotow. But now you ease farther back on the stick, right back into your lap, to achieve a 45-degree, nose-up attitude. That's when you begin to feel like an astronaut.

Now an odd thing happens: The speed *increases* as you pull back the stick. Weird. The reason is easily seen in autotow: Because of your angle, your flight path must cover a greater distance than the tow vehicle, in the same amount of time.

The best place for a tow hook is near the glider's center of gravity, and a plane so equipped is said to have a "CG" hook. It allows for a higher launch—somewhat more than half the length of the towline—so with a 2,000-foot line, for example, launch height will be perhaps 1,200 feet.

As you near that height, the cable begins to pull the nose down, and the ground slips into view. As the pressure increases, if you continue to hold the elevator the plane will begin to porpoise. So you anticipate that, and just beforehand, when the glider is about 80 degrees up from the vehicle or winch (and ordinarily when the winch operator reduces power), you ease forward on the stick, pull the release knob, then immediately place the nose of the glider below the horizon to eliminate the possibility of a stall.

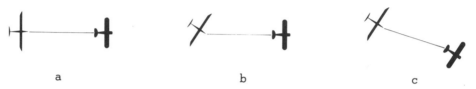

a   b   c

Cross-wind takeoff, with wind coming across the field from pilots' right. As planes begin to roll (a), sailplane pilot avoids weathervaning by turning his rudder as though to turn left. When he leaves the ground (b), he crabs to maintain position behind towplane parallel to runway. As soon as the towplane becomes airborne (c), the pilot allows his glider to drift to a position aligned with the towplane's heading.

As soon as the towplane lifts, though, you can start formation flying, following him and anticipating him, and, if you're not used to it, building up anxiety. Funny thing: most beginning sailplane pilots—even experienced power pilots—find tow technique horrendous; they get out of line, overcompensate to move back, overcompensate again, and find themselves whooshing back and forth, a 200-foot pendulum, until they hear the welcome words behind them: "I've got it."

One thing that will help is to avoid moving into the slipstream, the wash of turbulent air blowing back from the tow plane's propeller. You fly either below it (low-tow position) or above it (high tow). High tow is almost universally preferred in the United States for two reasons: (1) You're a little higher, so if the rope breaks you have more time to decide what to do, and (2) Americans believe that if the rope breaks on low tow, it may come back through the sailplane's windshield. Actually, it won't. At least I can find no record of it ever having done so—even in Australia, where low tow is used almost exclusively.

The best way to keep in high-tow position behind most towplanes is to fly

Glider must fly either a high-tow position . . .

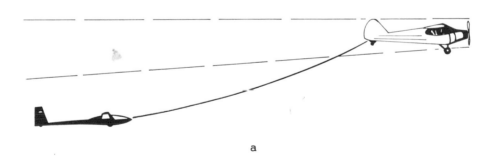

a

b

. . . or low-tow position (a), but not between the two (b), in the plane's wake.

your sailplane so that the tip of the towplane's tail lines up with the top of his wing. (Some instructors suggest that you line up the towplane's wings with the horizon. That's okay in Iowa, I suppose, but what do you do in the mountains of Idaho or in the dog-day mists of Virginia?)

Now—there is a controversy in tow technique that you should know about, and that is whether or not coordinated turns should be used. A few pilots still maintain that the rudder alone is sufficient, that a person being towed has enough to think about without having to worry about whether or not his turns are coordinated. That's probably true: You *can* steer the glider on tow with only the rudder; it yaws the sailplane and the towplane pulls it over. But in every other case in the whole sport of flying, such turning is dead wrong.

One strong advocate of coordinated turns is Tom Knauff, longtime instructor and owner of the Ridge Soaring Gliderport in Julian, Pennsylvania. "Using only the rudder works fine so long as nothing goes wrong," he says. "But suppose a pilot has a rope break and wants to turn around quickly to head back to the airport. Then the phenomenon of *negative habit transfer* appears. The cause of most fatal accidents is the pilot trying to turn the airplane with the rudder. What happens is that he's afraid to bank because he's relatively close to the ground, and so he tries to turn the aircraft with the rudder. That flings one wing forward and slows the other enough that it stalls, and the plane spins in. I say that those people who are steering on aerotow with the rudder alone are just not ready to switch from that wrong way of flying to a right way of flying instantly upon a rope break."

On aerotow, you should make coordinated turns both when you find yourself misaligned with the towplane and when the towplane is turning. When you see the towplane bank, you bank, too, trying to keep right on that turning radius. Don't cut across the circle or you'll develop a slack rope that may snap with a neck-wrench jerk when the slack disappears. On the other hand, don't fly too far out. Some students get the impression that they always should be directly behind the tail of the towplane, and so in a turn they try to fly outside the circle's diameter, and they must do so at a higher speed—which, when they return to the path, will lead again to slack.

A small amount of slack is nothing to worry about, particularly since most ropes today absorb shocks without springing. So the proper procedure in most cases is to do nothing, to simply hold your position and allow the towplane to take up the slack. But to guard against the possibility of the rope breaking when it jerks, the glider pilot should yaw his plane just before the rope straightens. It will then pull the craft straight, cushioning the shock as it does. If for some reason the slack is severe—if you see the rope looping down toward your landing gear—then release before it becomes entangled.

ROPE BREAKS

This really should be headed "aborted tow" or "premature release" or something, because it includes not only breaking towropes, but accidental release and purposeful release by the towplane. Your passenger, knocked about by turbulence, may reach out to steady himself by grabbing the release knob. Or the towplane may suddenly develop engine trouble: the pilot drops the towline to get out of your way.

Whatever the case, an unexpected release is extraordinarily confusing to a glider pilot, whether he's a tyro or an expert. And that period of momentary bafflement—coupled with a nose-high attitude, sudden loss of "thrust," and perhaps vortices as the glider settles into the towplane's wake—can very easily lead to a stall, and a spin into the ground. That's why it's so important to know what should be done and to practice rope breaks during training.

The key figure is 200. Below 200 feet you can't turn around. You must land ahead (or off to the side). And you should know what's out there. Racecar drivers often walk an unfamiliar track. A few sailplane pilots do the same; they take a leisurely stroll beyond the runway. The *least* one should do is to ask local pilots what is beyond the runway, and what they do if the rope breaks. Perhaps a big, soft field lies off to the left, hidden.

The majority of breaks occur at low altitudes, up to 50 feet or so. Two main things to remember here: First, get the nose down. A stall from 10 feet isn't going to kill you, but it will sure mess up the plane. Second, stop quickly. There have been cases in which the pilot has been so happy to land nicely after a rope break that he forgets to put on the brakes and rolls right into the fence at runway's end.

If the towplane has a problem—engine failure or fire or an ill pilot—and lands ahead of you, the proper procedure is for him to roll off the left side of the runway while you steer right. That won't work unless one of you has had the presence of mind to drop the rope. Because of that, some instructors teach their students to rest their left hand on their knee, ready to grab the release knob in case something goes wrong. Others, however, instruct students to keep their hand on the dive-brake lever, because if released before 200 feet, they'll probably want to get down quickly—or at least to be able to find the lever if it's wanted.

If a pilot tries to turn around with insufficient altitude, he'll do one of two things: stall and spin in, or touch a wing to the ground and cartwheel. Take your pick.

At about 200 feet (get the nose down) you can elect to turn around. You don't *have* to (if the towplane hasn't much power you may be too far from the airport by then), but you can. You may not want to if the wind is blowing more than 10 mph or so. But you can.

Which way to turn? Probably there's a crosswind. Turn into it, so you'll drift back toward the runway. Make the turn steep and coordinated. A 45-degree angle of bank will get you around quickest with the least danger. (Keep the yaw string straight.) Use at least pattern speed, plus a few miles for safety.

To be underlined in all glider pilots' minds: On each takeoff, *expect* the rope to break.

That same Tom Knauff is the inventor of the *200-foot holler*. Two hundred feet above the ground is the magical minimum point at which, under normal circumstances, you have room enough to turn around and head back to the field. If you're not monitoring altitude during tow (and that's one of the *last* things you'd otherwise think about) you'll waste valuable seconds determining just where you are. So Knauff has his students call out as they pass the 200-foot mark. If a student forgets, he suddenly finds that the towrope has been released from the back seat. He learns, and remembers. Sometimes, in late afternoon, when a Nimbus or an ASW-22 takes off for some soaring in the relaxed quiet of dusk, you know that the pilot was long ago taught the art of soaring by Tom Knauff, for from within the distant cockpit, even above the towplane's whine, comes a muffled voice: "Two-hunddreddd!"

Occasionally, signals are passed between towplane and glider. For example, when the towplane rolls his wings, the pilot wants the sailplane to release. He may be saying he's low on gas or is having engine trouble, but probably he's simply telling the pilot that high lift has been occurring in this spot all morning, and nothing better can be expected.

Soaring signals. (Soaring Society of America)

One way to sidestep the problem of launch is with a self-launching sailplane. This is the Finnish-made Eiri*Avion PIK-20. Engine (43 hp) lifts glider to soaring altitude, then is stopped and folded down into fuselage to reduce drag. Engine can also be cranked up into place and started in flight. Maximum L/D: 39.5:1 at 64 mph; minimum sink: 120 fpm at 48 mph; maximum speed: 174 mph. (Smitty's Soaring Service, Clinton, NY)

A less expensive launch method is leg power. This is the 100-pound fabric-and-wood ULF-1, designed and built by Dieter Reich and Heiner Neumann, and holding a German airworthiness certificate. It's designed to be launched from slopes of more than 20 degrees. After becoming airborne, pilot hauls in his legs so he can use the rudder pedals. Glide ratio: 14.5:1. Maximum speed: 112 mph.

If you spot a particularly luscious cloud and want to check it out, you can direct the towplane over there simply by moving so far to the side that his plane is turned in the proper direction.

If you tug on your release knob and nothing happens, you can tell him that, too. First, though, make sure you're pulling on the right thing. Aviation writer Linn Emrich, in his *Complete Book of Sky Sports*, tells of the time when, as a student, he got his controls confused. He was on tow, and when he yanked for release, the mechanism apparently failed. Not only that, but

. . . the whole glider seemed to be acting strangely. I had settled into the prop wash and was shuddering and wallowing along. Just about to bail out, I gave one insightful look at what I was doing. The "release knob," which my white-knuckled fingers were clutching, was plainly labeled "spoiler."

If you find that you really are pulling on the release knob and you're not being released, tell the tow pilot by moving far to the side so he can see you, and waggling your wings. (Point to the rope and shrug your shoulders, too, though that isn't in the rule book.) He'll understand, and slowly and gently make a big sweep to the runway approach, and when you're lined up, he'll release you. Don't worry about that dangling rope; you'll hardly feel that it's there.

Camera mounted on a wing boom and triggered remotely captures a Schweizer 1-26, the United States' most popular sailplane, just after release. (Photo equipment courtesy of The Camera Shop, State College, PA)

But that situation almost never happens. Usually the release is smooth and uneventful. Look around to check for other aircraft, pull the release knob (red in United States planes, yellow in European), *twice* (to make sure) and as you hear and see the yellow plastic rope spring away, turn off gently to the right as the towplane drops off to the left, dangling the towrope behind him back to the field. Some pilots work it so they're rising as they release, to gain a few more feet of altitude. This is probably a poor practice. Better would be to *lower* the nose upon release. If your habitual release response is to push forward on the stick, then if sometime the rope breaks or you accidentally pull the release knob, you may tend to push forward instead of pulling back, a more natural reaction.

As you release, look again for other aircraft (a plane that apparently is standing still is on a collision course with you), then shift into your favorite lolling-about speed, sigh, let your shoulders drop, and relax.

Chapter Seven

Coming Down

Two things are useless: the runway behind you and the air above you.
World War II glider-pilot saying

Eventually, no matter what you do, you'll have to land. Almost all sailplane students are scared silly during those first few landings—and, I suppose, with good cause. Things happen relatively fast, there's much to think about, and you can't ram in the throttle to go around again if you make a mistake.

But landing a sailplane isn't as difficult as it seems. Most sailplanes—and all training gliders—are extremely forgiving; it's relatively difficult to stall them, easy to guide them, and they land at a slow speed—30 to 40 mph or so—and in only about 200 feet on runways usually ten times that length. They're tougher than you think, too, and will absorb a much higher landing shock than their looks indicate. And their capabilities are wide: You can come in extremely steep or shallow and still be on a good glide path.

On the other hand, landings, *planned* landings, are where about half of all serious accidents happen. And a strange thing: The new pilot isn't the one who has those accidents; it's the overconfident license holder. Among power pilots you hear the expression, "Beware the hundred-hour pilot," the person who has flown enough to have lost that concentration, has become so confident he neglects safety. A similar saying might be "Beware the hundred-flight sailplane pilot," who no longer believes it will happen to *him*. Tony Doharty, Schweizer's sales manager, calls such overconfidence "rapture of the heights." It's so *easy* to fly a sailplane that a pilot sometimes loses that keen edge of anticipation.

But a student certainly has apprehension, and one thing that worries him is that he'll become so interested in trying to stay in a thermal that before he knows it he has drifted downwind so far he'll not be able to return to the field. That probably won't happen (a student's natural conservatism won't allow him to go that far), but one way of setting the mind at rest is to work only upwind from the airport. Another trick is taught to gliding students by Salem, New Hampshire, instructor Don Brasseur. If you look out of the cockpit at a 45-degree angle, the distance from the spot you see to the point right under the plane is whatever it says on your altimeter. You know how far you can glide, so you can approximate your margin—tempered, of course, by the direction and velocity of the wind and whatever in the way of lift or sink you encounter. Think of a huge funnel sitting on the runway, its spout 600 feet long (the height at which you start your pattern) and its sides representing your glide slope. (Except in calm weather, the funnel will be quite out-of-round.) A similar technique is used by Dayton, Ohio, sailplane pilot Marvin Frost. He uses his index finger, held horizontally about 6 inches from his eye, to estimate a 10:1 glide slope. He lines up his finger's top edge with the horizon, and if he can see the runway below the bottom of his finger, he knows that he can make it even though his L/D drops to 10.

If you don't know what that means, I guess that this is the time to learn, because you'll need to think in those terms to judge your landings. L/D (pronounced "L over D") is the lift-drag ratio, and, obviously, is the lift that the wings are producing divided by the drag the aircraft is generating. The result exactly equals the glide ratio. If a plane is said to have a glide ratio of 25 to 1 (25:1), that means that when the L/D is at its optimum, the plane will glide 25 feet forward for every foot that it descends. So on a calm day with everything perfect, a pilot at 4,000 feet can expect to glide almost 19 miles if he encounters neither thermals nor sink (downward-moving air). The higher the glide ratio, of course, the better the performance of the aircraft. Trainers have a glide ratio of about 20:1, while competition sailplanes often are in excess of 45:1. (For comparison, a Piper Cub J3C-65 has a 10:1 glide ratio, while a Rogallo sailwing hang glider has an L/D of about 5:1.)

The term *sink* when applied to a sailplane (rather than to the air) indicates how fast it will drop in its rated glide ratio. Know the sink, check the altitude, and you can figure roughly how long you can stay up. A sink rate of 2 feet per second, for example, means that a tow to 3,000 feet in still air could result in a flight of about 1,500 seconds, or 25 minutes. It also means that in a strong updraft—1,000 fpm is not that rare—a sailplane can easily surpass the climb rate of a small power plane.

The difference between L/D and sink figures continues to confuse many power pilots, but if you're a soaring enthusiast the concepts quickly sort themselves out. For example, the L/D rate of a Schweizer 1-26, America's most popular sailplane, is 23:1 at 45 mph, while the lowest sink rate, 2.6 fps, is found at 38 mph. Therefore, when you're circling inside a thermal, you'll want to keep the speed at as close to 38 mph as you can, the lowest sink rate. (It has to be a little above that because you're banking.) When the thermal runs out and you've entered bad air, you want to whip through it fast, so you'd push the speed to at least 45 mph, losing a little altitude, but getting to that next thermal quickly. (More about that in next chapter.)

The approach and landing itself are part judgment, part instrument monitoring. Note that that's *instrument*, not *instruments*, because during the pattern, the only gauge you look at is your airspeed indicator. Time was when instructors taught by altitude: "Enter pattern at xxx feet, turn into base at xxx, start final at xxx." No longer. They found that some pilots got so used to monitoring their altimeter they forgot common sense. One experienced Massachusetts pilot was landing at a field in a nearby state when those watching from the clubhouse noticed that he entered his landing pattern a little low. They expected him to cut short his downwind leg (see page 86), but he traveled on and on, following the conventional path. As he turned into the final, he was treetop high, *much* lower than usual—but with his highest L/D, he could just about make it. Instead, out slid his dive brakes, and as gently as a landing goony bird he settled into the young pines a couple of hundred feet down from the runway. Didn't get hurt and, miraculously, neither did his plane. Just his ego.

His altimeter, set for sea level, was correct. But he had forgotten that his home airport was nearly a hundred feet lower than this runway, and though the landing didn't *look* right to him, he said later, he trusted his instruments.

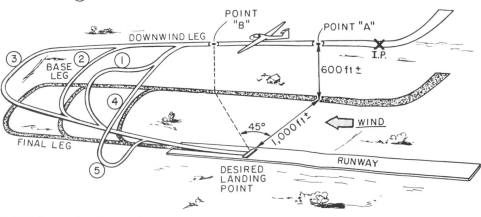

① "TOO HIGH" PATH
② HALF DIVE BREAKS
③ NO DIVE BREAKS
④ FULL DIVE BREAKS
⑤ FISHHOOK (WRONG)

POINT "B"
POINT "A"
DOWNWIND LEG
I.P.
③ ② ①
BASE LEG
600 ft ±
④
45°
1,000 ft ±
WIND
FINAL LEG
RUNWAY
⑤
DESIRED LANDING POINT

A 180-degree landing pattern.

That's one reason why most instructors now teach a variation of what Tom Knauff, in his *Glider Basics—From First Flight to Solo*, calls the TLAR technique, which stands for "That Looks About Right." The routine relies on judgment—not of altitude, but of *angles*. Human beings are very poor at judging altitude. (Biologically, why should it be any different?) Research shows that above 500 feet the magnitude of error in judging altitude is about 30 percent; at 1,000 feet the average pilot would guess anything between 700 and 1,300 feet. Binocular vision (the comparison of the spread of the eyes focused at a distant object) coupled with an interpretation of the degree of flatness of the eye lens and the angle involved, is okay up to perhaps a couple of hundred feet. Beyond that, human beings must rely on memory to compare the apparent size of an object with what is remembered as its true size. Not very accurate, particularly when you're looking at trees from the top instead of the side. And particularly when you're flying in Colorado and trying to compare balsams to New Jersey maples—or in the desert, when all you can see is sage and yucca.

But at judging *angles*, particularly a 45-degree angle, we're pretty good. We're used to dealing in angles. We look at a stake in the ground 100 feet away and we know its distance not only because of its size (it could be a fence post), and not only because of our binocular vision (the few inches between the eyes doesn't give much separation), but because our eyes are maybe 5 feet from the ground, and we're looking downward at a subconsciously recognized angle.

But we know neither the *figures* for that angle nor the mathematical relationship between that 5 feet from the ground and the distance to the object. And without training (or at least thinking about it), we can't easily extrapolate that 5 feet to 500 feet so that we can use it in flying.

What the sailplane pilot has to do, then, is think in terms of flight paths, and one way of learning that is to practice on the ground. A Schweizer trainer 2-33, with full dive brakes on, drops at a glide ratio of 5:1. To give an idea of what this really means, some instructors are having their students pace it off on the field. If a student's eyes are about 5 feet from the ground, and if a 2-33 glides 5 feet forward for every foot it drops, that would mean that a miniature 2-33—dive brakes fully open—would glide from the student's eyes to a spot 25 feet in front of him. (The student should pace off the distance, then look at the landing spot sideways, over his shoulder, as though he were landing, and as reinforcement he should point to it.)

With dive brakes closed, that same plane floats along in calm air at an L/D of 20:1. Now the model glider's landing spot would be 100 feet away, and the view is through a 3-degree angle.

That 20:1 is an amazing thing to recognize for the first time. It's even more amazing up in the sky. In fact, it's so amazing that most people just can't believe the figures, just can't believe they can float *that far*. And that's why more people overshoot a runway than undershoot it, why most off-field landings result from overshooting runways. At one Eastern sailplane field, somebody lands too long, far down the 3,500-foot runway, almost every busy day. But out of about 40,000 landings in the five years the field has been open, only one pilot has landed short. (And he did it twice.)

The best ratio on approach, logically enough, is about halfway between the extreme glide paths, or in a 2-33, 12:1—about 60 feet in front of those eyes at the 5-foot level.

Those are the three critical L/D ratios—at full dive brakes, no dive brakes, and about halfway between—and every so often a student should pace off the distances and look at them, imagining himself in the landing pattern.

And when he has the angles set in mind, what does he do with them? Here is a typical landing sequence, using essentially the TLAR technique:

The INITIAL POINT, or IP (see page 86 again), is the spot on the landing pattern where the pilot says, "Okay, now I'm set in my pattern." It's on the downwind leg, and it's ordinarily a couple of hundred feet upwind from a line extending over from the touchdown point. The IP may or may not be the pattern entry point (PEP), but often it is, and it's also often thought of as where the pattern begins. The pilot arranges things (with dive brakes or an extra S turn or two) so that at the IP, the sailplane is at an altitude of 600 feet, at most airports. Since this is the last time the altimeter is to be used, the pilot should tap it to make sure it isn't sticking.

The prudent pilot always flies at least a 180-degree pattern, for each leg gives him information. The pattern approach allows him to check the sock, look for other landing pilots, and glance at the runway to see if anything is on it. The downwind leg gives him an opportunity to get a fix on the wind speed and direction; he knows by how much he must crab and by how fast the earth is moving under him. He is also low enough now to see the spot where he will touch down. The base leg gives him a better idea of glide slope, and presents a fine view to verify that the landing area is clear of planes, children, vehicles, and cows. If not, now is the time to choose a slightly different landing spot—short, long, on another runway, on the taxiway, whatever.

And on the final, of course, the whole thing comes together.

Back at the IP again, the beginning pilot does four things (and should memorize them):

1. *Put hand on the dive-brake handle*. Eventually, every pilot tries to vary his descent rate by pulling his release knob or trim handle. This step helps delay the day. Crack the brakes open to test them.

2. *Establish pattern speed*. Pattern speed is 150 percent of stall speed plus half the groundwind speed plus a few mph if the pilot suspects turbulence. In a 2-33, for instance, the stall speed (dual) is 33. Add half again to that, and you arrive at about 50 mph—a figure a 2-33 pilot should brand onto his brain. If the wind is blowing at 10 mph, add half of that (5 mph) to the landing speed, and if it's gusty, add perhaps another 3 mph. That totals about 58—say 60 mph. It may be a few mph higher than some instructors would figure, but I'd rather see a new pilot run his pattern at a slightly faster clip than to see him just hanging in there. Speed doesn't kill (often); its lack does. One reason for a pattern speed that seems at first glance to be excessive is something called the *wind gradient*. The wind near the ground, because of friction, moves more slowly than the wind at altitude, so that if the air is moving at 30 mph at 800 feet, it may be blowing at only 10 mph at an altitude of 25 feet. So if you're coming in at something just above stall speed and the wind suddenly drops by 20 mph, you're in trouble.

The pattern speed should have been figured earlier, of course, and *established* at the IP.

3. *Note speed of descent,* and if it isn't the normal rate of about 200 fpm, adjust it with the dive brakes. (Look at this instrument on the downwind leg only.)

4. *Disregard altimeter*. When you've gone past the IP, you won't look at the altimeter again. In fact, after you've checked your rate of descent, you won't look inside the cockpit again except for quick glimpses of your speed. (Some instructors slap a cover over the altimeter face.) This leg goes fast because wind is blowing you along.

POINT A (see diagram again) is the spot on your downwind leg that's opposite the touchdown point. Some instructors have their students call out "Point A" as they pass it, to make sure the student's mind is on the touchdown point. The pilot should keep watching that point through most of the pattern, removing his eyes only to check speed, yaw string, and, of course, other gliders and field activity.

POINT B is somewhat down the leg from Point A. It's the place from which the touchdown point looks like it's at a 45-degree angle from the path of the plane. Sing out "Point B" and impress your instructor. You don't do anything here but *get ready* to turn. The reason a big deal is made of the point is that you can easily recognize a 45-degree angle; you probably couldn't recognize the 39-degree angle (or whatever it might be) where you turn into base.

. . . LIKE THE BACK OF YOUR HAND you should have total familiarity with your cockpit and everything in it. Here's a good exercise: While on the ground, close your eyes and imagine going through a complete flight. Start with the cockpit check, touching each instrument, control, knob, and lever in turn. Go through signals to wingman, takeoff, boxing the prop wash, release, a few gentle and steep turns, a stall or two, and perhaps a spin. Toss in a couple of emergencies, and maybe a maneuver or two you wouldn't try in the air. Then come in for a landing. You'll be surprised at what you learn.

TURN ONTO BASE LEG. This is a big decision in the landing process—*when* to make this turn. Remember that at IP you were at 600 feet. On a calm day with no dive brakes and a 20:1 L/D, you could sail on for a mile on this leg, then turn around and come back, and you'd make it with room to spare. But you want to time it so that you'll be coming into final at about midpoint in the L/D for your plane, so anywhere after passing that steepest L/D (5:1) is okay. The exact point isn't critical because you can easily adjust for an error. Try *not* to memorize where to turn by noting landmarks, because they won't be at the next field. And every time you land you should be honing judgment that will serve well when you're coming in to a strange airport or in a field of alfalfa.

One thing that is particularly important to remember in this and the final turn, and throughout the whole pattern: Keep the yaw string straight. No matter how good the pilot, in time of trouble, in a high-pressure situation when he realizes that he's getting dangerously low, his instincts tell him to kick the plane around with the rudder—and that's dead wrong. That's why stalls happen, and that's why so many serious accidents occur on planned landings. Keep the yaw string straight and you'll not overrudder.

ON THE BASE LEG, the pilot makes the final judgment as to how things look—TLAR, he hopes. If he finds that he is somewhere in that huge cone between 5:1 and 20:1, he'll continue on, holding speed and adjusting descent rate with the dive brakes: Pull the lever back, and out slides the brakes, causing high sink, low L/D; push it forward, he decreases sink, lands long.

You strive to keep the speed steady because you want the pitch attitude of the plane constant; if you vary the speed between, say, 50 and 55 mph, the nose—and horizon—will be bouncing up and down.

If you find you're much too high as you go into the base leg, you can make a right-hand turn, then left again—in effect extending the downwind leg. Power pilots sometimes make what's called a "buttonhook" or "fishhook" turn, an extension of the base leg, then a sharp U-turn back, and finally a right-hand turn into final. (See page 86 again.) That may be okay with a surge of power standing at ready, but it can be suicide with a glider—despite what you might read elsewhere. What happens is that the pilot finds that he is not quite as high as he thought, and that the sharp fishhook turn is happening lower than he'd like. His temptation, once again, is to avoid turning steeply, because subconsciously he's afraid of touching a wing tip to the ground—even though he's nowhere near the surface. To get around that turn as fast as possible, he tends to use more and more rudder, in an attempt to *skid* around. And go into a skid he does, presenting the side of the plane to the relative wind, increasing drag and losing even more height. Meanwhile, because of the overbanking tendency brought about by too much rudder, he's trying to compensate by applying opposite aileron. By this time the plane has lost almost all of its lift, and so in a last frantic attempt the pilot pulls back on the stick to clear the fence at the end of the runway. Stall.

TURN TO FINAL should be sharp—45 degrees or so—as was the turn to base. The making of steep pattern turns should become habitual; the steeper the turn, the smaller the temptation to overrudder. Derek Piggot, one of the most respected sailplane writers, points out that if you attempt to stall most gliders in a turn of 30-degree bank or more, you can't pull the wing up to a stall position without pulling back on the stick *violently*—an unlikely thing to do in a critical situation. The FAA has something to say about turns, too: "It is much safer, if one error or the other must be made, to slip in a steep turn than to skid in a flat turn."

ON FINAL you should be closely monitoring your speed, keeping it constant, keeping your eye on your touchdown point; if you're coming in correctly (and if you've had enough landing experience that you're relaxed enough to notice), that touchdown spot shouldn't move. If it does drift upward, you're undershooting; if it slides downward, you're landing long. Don't try to aim for the touchdown point with your elevator. (If you're *much* too high, you can increase sink by side slipping, as on page 91.)

ROUNDOUT AND TOUCHDOWN. Some pilots, even in crosswinds, can consistently land on a square the size of a card table. One Sunday afternoon a club near Philadelphia held a contest to see who could land closest to a marker. Three sailplanes touched down within 19 inches of it.

Touchdown is easy if you use your dive brakes as a touchdown control, and if you look not at the ground underneath you, but at the far end of the field. As you near the surface, your approach should be shallow, so that you have a smooth, easy *roundout*—the point at which you, by easing back on the stick, switch from an angled glide path to one virtually paralleling the runway. If the glide path is steep, the roundout timing will be critical, and you'll be more likely to *balloon*, to bounce up from the runway without even having touched it. You

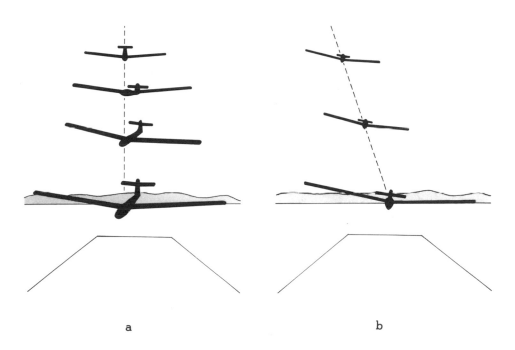

a   b

Two kinds of slips—forward and side—are used in landing. The forward slip (a), is useful to steepen the angle of descent beyond the maximum afforded by fully open spoiler or dive brakes. It is used to land short over an obstacle, or when the pilot misjudges and comes in excessively high. It is affected by banking and yawing so that as the plane approaches over the normal ground track (centered over an extension of the runway's midline), its side is exposed to the relative wind, inducing increased drag.

A side-slip landing (b) is usually used to counteract a crosswind, but it can also steepen descent. In that case, the final glide is begun so that the nose is pointing parallel to the runway, but the plane is actually off somewhat to the downwind side. The wing on the runway side is lowered, and the plane slips toward the runway, presenting its side to the wind.

might even do a stall landing—perhaps okay for power planes, but a sailplane, with its light wing loading, could waft up to stall 5 feet above the runway. Crunch.

So come in low, perform a gentle roundout, and if you're a little early and quite a distance from the touchdown point, you can skim along the surface using what's called "ground effect." The faster your speed, the longer the glider floats before touchdown.

Just before you reach the point where you want to touch down, pull on the dive brakes (not all the way, or your wheel brake will be on) as you ease back on the stick more and more until gently you sink, mushily smooth, into the ground.

LANDING OUT

To someone who has never made an off-field landing, the very idea is horrendous. It's not all that dangerous: Landing speed is lower than with most power planes, the ship itself is lighter, has less chance of digging into soft earth, the single wheel lends itself more readily to rough fields (you have only half the chance of hitting a rock), there's more time to get ready for a landing than you probably think, and most soaring pilots know more about landings than power pilots do anyway.

The big unknown is the human reception. One Nevada pilot, landing almost in the center of a cocktail party, was greeted with an invitation to dinner. On the other hand, California pilot George Asdel once touched down in a nuclear-weapons storage yard where he was met by machine guns.

Planes do crash on off-field attempts, of course, and the causes narrow to three:

1. The pilot waits too long to make the decision to land.
2. He executes a poor approach and touchdown.
3. He encounters such hidden obstructions as woodchuck holes.

You can't do much about the chuck holes. Otherwise, the factors are totally in your control.

One way to prepare yourself is simply to think. On boring automobile trips, particularly in hilly regions, imagine yourself suddenly forced to land. Select a field in the distance, then check out your choice when you get near enough to see the surface.

Do the same thing from the air. Next time you're thermaling around the airport, make believe you must land somewhere other than on the runway. Where would you set down? From which direction? Later, walk the area to check your judgment. You might also practice actual landings in remote sections of your home field, having beforehand walked the surface.

Out on a cross-country soar, if you haven't had much outlanding experience, start looking for landing spots whenever you drop below 3,000 feet. Some pilots say that if you're a relative newcomer, never leave the area of a specific landing site once you've dipped below 2,500 AGL. You have 1,500 feet to find lift, and if you do, be off. If not, get ready to land. In that way you'll never be caught unprepared.

What kind of a field are you looking for (other than big)? *Avoid* fields that are:

• *Sloping.* Any slant that you can see from 1,000 feet up is too steep for an ideal landing. In particular, you should never land downhill, because you'll overshoot. Cross-hill

Bernard Fetchett, 1979 British Open champion, runs out of lift on a cross-country trip and sets his Vega down in a newly harvested field.

landings are possible, but tricky. Uphill landings are best, but if your glide path is as usual, the impact could be jarring.

• *In the lee of hills.* If the day is windy, you may find turbulence or unexpected sink.

• *With obstructions near the approach end.* Objects in the way—wires, trees, houses, fences—reduce the field length by at least ten times the height of the obstruction. Wires are particularly bad: You may not be able to see them. Look for poles rather than wires. Avoid fields where the approach is across a highway; most surfaced roads are lined with telephone poles. Never attempt to go under a wire. You're not that good.

The best surface is that of a large polo field without the horses. Lacking that, look for newly planted cropland, which is usually devoid of rocks, holes, stumps, and other hazards. Irrigation or drainage ditches usually can be seen. Plowed land should be avoided; if it can't be, land *with* the furrows.

Landing in cropland should be avoided because (1) the farmer will be upset, and (2) the plane could be severely damaged, and (3) so could you. Beneath that crop could lurk ditches, logs, sprinkler systems. And the crop itself can catch a wing or break off a stabilizer, or even cause a nose-over. Corn is particularly hazardous. Pasture lands are also poor because of generally rough surfaces dotted with stumps, trees, ruts, and rocks, to say nothing of cows.

Check for wind direction by noting smoke, flags, clotheslines, blowing dust or snow, waves in crops, or ripples on ponds and lakes (smooth on upwind ends). Cloud shadows give a general indication, but shouldn't be trusted.

A normal landing pattern is essential. This is no time for improvisation. The only exception is that the pattern should be a full 360 degrees to give you time for a thorough check of the field.

Coming Down 93

Ignore your altimeter, of course (its information is useless), and once you've committed yourself to land, do so; don't try to take advantage of lift you might encounter in the pattern. Keep your eye on the intended landing spot; glance away and you might lose track of where you're going.

If you are landing upslope, come in with a little excess speed so that you can raise the nose a bit as you touch down. If you find that you're landing across a slope, try to come in on an uphill diagonal, then land more or less in a shallow bank at touchdown, wings parallel to the slope.

To stop quickly, touch down at a slow speed, then push the stick full forward to force the glider up on its nose skid. If you've really screwed up and see that you're going to overshoot, what you do depends on what's at the field's end. A solid wall? Better ground-loop: Determine your plan from the air, and land as slowly as possible, then touch the wing tip to the ground, and apply full rudder to swivel the plane around. It will damage the craft, but probably not you. If the plane starts to flip over, push the control stick away from your stomach, pull your knees up, hold your head down, and wrap your arms about yourself.

If you're going to run into a fence, aim for a post. It will fall flat, pulling the wire down with it. You can ride over the top. If you run into woods, steer between the trees. Your wings ripping off will cushion your halt.

Will the farmer be upset? Rarely, says sailplane safety expert Steve du Pont, "if you look thankful enough and scared enough." Fort Collins, Colorado, pilot Clay Thomas says he carries a bottle of champagne with him for just such emergencies. "Believe me," he says, "I have seen many an irate farmer's rage transformed to joy."

Chapter Eight

Staying Up

Here at the bottom of the atmospheric ocean, like inhabitants of some two-dimensional Flatland, the human species is preoccupied with movement horizontally. As a result, most people rarely look up, and except for occasionally acknowledging sunsets, rainbows, and a rare thunderhead, few note that there even *is* a sky.

There are exceptions. Meteorologists, of course, and cowboys, and those who live on mountaintops. And, to some extent, pilots, parachutists, and balloonists. But power-plane pilots are concerned mainly with storm clouds. Parachutists are interested only in a column of air the width of a silo. And to a balloonist, the only part of the atmosphere that matters is the bubble of wind in which he floats.

But a sailplane pilot, if he's a good one, takes the sky *personally*. He constantly is feeling the air for nearly subliminal currents of lift, and glorying in them when he finds them. His domain stretches out for miles, sometimes for as far as he can see. The clouds shout their information; the ground, far below, whispers; the plane itself hints—and all tell him about the atmospheric fabric through which he must travel.

Air is continually streaming upward and sinking, throughout the day and into the night—a cycle of heating, expanding, rising, cooling, stagnating, then sinking, to be heated again. But it ordinarily produces few obvious clues to reveal what is really going on. Meanwhile, obscuring even the hints are breezes —not blowing evenly, but in waves, in fits and spurts, invisible unless revealed as undulations on a barley field, or as rain sheeting the sea. The surface of the earth shapes the wind, shapes the weather itself, deflecting it, swirling it, roiling and bubbling it, like rocks on a mountainside influencing a gushing stream.

A sailplane pilot can't see the flow, but he may be able to sort out the signs: The cottony cloud tops that speak of thermals. The smoothly curved len-ticular clouds, high to the lee of mountains, telling, with their eerily stacked shelf fungus, of waves. Circling birds. Drifting smoke. Nibbles and shudders and bumps of the plane as it makes its way through mile-high churnings. A pilot can find such basics in a book, but unless he learns to have a *sense* of the sky, learns to use his sailplane almost like an aerial divining rod, he'll remain mediocre.

The nice thing about it is that even the rawest beginner learns the essen-tials quickly, learns first that there *is* something going on out there, and then learns to figure out what is happening—a whole body of knowledge largely ig-nored by power pilots. The new sailplane pilot quickly learns to feel for a ther-mal, then to center on it. He discovers that to hold it he must turn in a circle that is damn near perfect—no slipping, no sliding, no cockeyed yaw string—and so he learns to make smooth, coordinated, *precise* turns. He learns, too, the limits of his plane, learns exactly where it stalls, because a sailplane pilot, thermaling at minimum sinking speed, is always teasing a stall's thin edge. And when, as a stu-dent, he can't hold on to it, when unsuspected bumps of turbulence drop him out a few times, he learns how to react swiftly and correctly, a reaction that could someday save his life.

Robert Buck, an ex-senior captain at TWA, tells about how his fifteen-year-old son, after one of his first sailplane lessons, relived at the dinner table the recovery from an incipient stall. Says Buck: "Now when he hears the sound drop and feels the controls loosen and shoves forward without even looking at the air speed, I know he is getting the word. Which was one reason I wanted my son to start his flying in a glider. I think he'll appreciate the slow part of flight, the part that can hurt you if not understood; I think he'll respect it, not fear it, and be able to handle it, and above all he will understand."

The essence of soaring, of course, is to get high, and the only way to do that (other than to be towed up there) is to climb up on rising currents of air. Of the different kinds of atmospheric conditions that cause these upward movements of air, only three are in widespread use: ridge, thermal, and wave lift.

RIDGE LIFT

When something blocks the path of wind—a cliff or a mountain or even a wide building—the wind is deflected around and over the top. If a sailplane is in the rising air—the *orographic* lift, it's called—and if the movement upward is faster than the aircraft's sink rate, then the plane will rise. Not too surprising, but a staggering discovery for those early men in their gliding machines who, when launched from a windblown hilltop, first found themselves going up instead of gliding down.

One good thing about ridge lift: You can usually depend on it. If a brisk wind is coming from a direction perpendicular to a ridge, you *know* that there's lift there. It might be enhanced by thermal activity or confused by upwind mountains, but that there's useful lift there is almost certain. And if the wind holds, you can glide as far as the ridge runs. Both the men's and women's world out-and-return records (1,016 and 637 miles) were acquired largely with the help of the prevailing westerlies vaulting the Appalachians (see next chapter). You may not be able to get very high with ridge lift, so you might want to use it simply to daw-

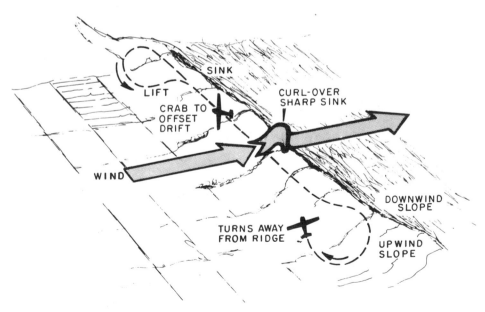

Ridge lift.

dle around until something better comes along, as a steppingstone to thermals—and then, sometimes, to waves.

A wind of about 10 or 20 mph is usually the minimum needed for good ridge soaring. It should strike the hill (which should be at least 800 feet high) within about 30 degrees of perpendicular. Generally a gentle slope (20 to 45 degrees) is better than a craggy cliff, because then the air tends to flow up smoothly, with little lift-destroying turbulence. Under moderate conditions, you can figure on rising perhaps half again as high as the ridge—under excellent conditions, perhaps three times as high. (Occasionally, during early evening hours, a stable layer of air is overlaid by a sharp temperature inversion, and a sailplane may be able to soar several thousand feet above the ridge. But those days are rare.)

How can you find the best ridge lift? Ask a dozen pilots and you'll get a dozen answers. One, for example: From a point three quarters up the upwind side of a hill, draw an imaginary line upward at an angle of about 55 degrees, slanting toward the wind. Now extend or broaden that line to both sides, along the ridge, and fly as close to the result as you can.

Perhaps a better idea is simply to ask local sailplane pilots where best lift usually occurs, or follow the hawks. My own secret: *Visualize* what the air might be doing, then forget all the advice and trust your instincts.

Additional points that may or may not affect the lift:

• Because of the difference in surface friction, slopes covered with grass or snow produce much finer lift than those surfaced with woods.

• The height to which a plane can go in ridge lift doesn't necessarily increase with wind speed. Often high wind speed simply means more turbulence.

• When you encounter an area of strong sink, lower the nose immediately to get through it as soon as possible. Meantime, try to figure out the reason for that sink. Maybe the corollary will be helpful: The wind striking *that* ground feature, that promontory at *that* angle, should be producing good lift.

• Usually, as soon as you get downwind of the crest of the hill you move into drastically sinking air—dangerous, and to be avoided. But occasionally, isolated mountain peaks produce *rising* currents in their lee. The wind does a kind of loop as it passes the top, then continues ascending. Such a phenomenon can sometimes be seen on high peaks by a "smoking mountain" or "cap" cloud. Start upwind of the lacy tendrils of cloud, and you may lift high above it.

• Sometimes you can tell if a ridge is working by noting the ripples and undulations of the foliage. Writer Linn Emrich says that he can tell from his airport whether or not there's lift on a 3,000-foot-high ridge five miles away. Says he: "The upslope wind makes the alder and maple leaves turn over, and the undersides have a silvery shimmer that is visible for miles."

Sometimes ridge lift will stop, will simply shut off for no apparent reason. In at least one area the cause is a mountain that is upwind. Suddenly, because the airflow direction or speed has slightly shifted, air starts to pour down on the ridge, temporarily (or maybe for the rest of the day) damping out any lift. If the pilot is flying low at the time of cancellation, he may be in trouble. Suggestion: If the day seems to offer that possibility, fly high or fly fast or fly high and fast, but never low and slow.

• Occasionally, too, lift will be produced *behind* an isolated hill, where air that blows around the sides meets again.

When you run out of ridge, turn back *into* the wind. You'll stay in rising air, even though it may not be rising fast enough to lift you up. If you turn toward the hill, you may find two sets of problems:

1. You could pass the crest of the wave-form (in the lee) and enter considerable sink.

2. Because the wind adjacent to the ground often is traveling faster, if you turn toward the hill you may be swinging into turbulence. To pick up speed, you must shove your nose down—and by the time your speed picks up to normal, you may be brushing the treetops. For example, if you increase the airspeed from 40 to 60 mph in a 1-26, you will drop nearly 300 feet. Now add another factor: Because of the irregularities of the surface—saddles, outcroppings, smaller crests—eddies might be moving *horizontally*, most confusing to an inexperienced pilot. Further, airflow patterns at treetop level are usually retarded and much less laminar; a turbulent gust might stall you out, and that's one thing you don't want. Turn *away* and you may sink, but you won't crash.

For safety's sake, too, the rules of right-of-way must be strictly adhered to on the ridge. When two planes are heading toward each other in any situation, each should steer to the right (just as on the highway). But on a ridge, the sailplane with the ridge on his left should give way twice as far as usual. If the other pilot must yield, he may be forced into the mountain or into its lee. Another rule: If one sailplane *overtakes* another, he should pass between the first craft and the ridge, so that if the first plane starts a turn, there is no possibility of collision. (Away from ridges, the rules state, the overtaking sailplane should pass to the other plane's *right*.) And one more rule: Avoid passing directly over or under another plane.

At any rate, sailing on ridge lift (called "ridge running" when going for distance) is where many pilots hone their control techniques, flying back and forth, back and forth. In ideal conditions, in fact, one can stay up as long as his biological functions will allow. In the early years, flyers were intent mainly on breaking the stay-aloft record. But when contestants began to fly around the clock, and then throughout the night and into the next day, it became apparent that what was being tested was endurance, not skill.

THERMALS

When you're ridge soaring and looking for thermals, you can spot them in at least three different ways: (1) You feel a surge of lift that is unexpected, stronger than usual, and prolonged. That could very well be a thermal. Or (2) a young, sharp-edged cloud comes drifting over you; chances are, air is rising into it, so if you feel good lift where logically the rising air should be, bank into a tight circle and try to follow it up. Or (3) you *see* it coming up the ridge; trees start to thrash, dust and leaves begin to rise, and maybe a bird is circling above the confusion on unmoving wings. When the disturbance reaches you, check to see that no other plane is close, then lean your aircraft into a circle. If others are on the ridge, turn into the wind, adjust for lowest sink, and proceed outward in S curves with slow deliberation so nobody is confused as to what you're doing. When you're far enough away, try to climb into that thermal.

Thermals today are taken for granted. To a sailplane pilot the idea of air rising upward seems logical, commonplace, obvious. But in the early part of the century, nobody knew quite what to make of them, for if you're used to air moving only in a horizontal plane—and most nonpilots still are—the idea of a vertical wind is foreign.

FIRST TO FULFILL THE "C" REQUIREMENT
 From Fred C. Kelly's *The Wright Brothers*,
 a biography authorized by Orville Wright

Shortly after his arrival at Montgomery, Alabama, early in 1910, Orville Wright had a new experience in the air. While at an altitude of about 1,500 feet, he found himself unable to descend, even though the machine was pointed downward as much as seemed safe. . . . He didn't know what to make of this. For nearly five minutes he stayed there in a puzzled state of mind bordering on alarm. Later it occurred to him that the machine must have been in a rising air current of unusual diameter, and that doubtless he could have quickly returned to earth if he had first steered horizontally to get away from the rising current.

What does a thermal look like? Nobody knows for sure. Nevertheless, I can see two of them from where I sit right now. In the corner of my study, an Aladdin space heater is removing the spring chill. The heated air is rising past a window, and the outside scene is shifting through the waving currents. Up near the ceiling a spiderweb jiggles in the breeze. And on the opposite wall, sunlight is casting wavy undulations. All that is a thermal, or at least the effects of one.

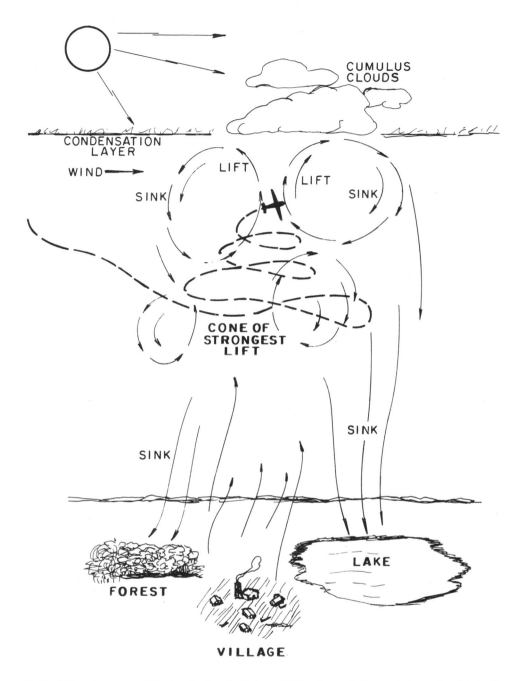

Dotted line shows possible track of sailplane as it flies through thermal, turns back into it, then centers and spirals upward.

I see the other thermal when I look out of the window along the top of an asphalt road. Even though the day is cold, bright sunlight has been warming the road all morning, and now the asphalt is releasing heat into the air above it, which rises shimmering and waving like the air above my heater. That's a thermal, too, and in theory a sailplane pilot could skim along that road, using it—well, like a highway.

But lift from a road is thin and unreliable. What the sailplane pilot looks for are thermals consisting of huge, swift-rising blobs of heated air that he can get into and wallow around in and still be blown sky-high. Such thermals, from many sources, start when a section of the landscape—a newly plowed field, for instance—gets heated by the sun. The field, in turn, heats the air immediately above it, causing the air to expand and to become lighter than the surrounding, cooler air. The air also becomes lighter if, because of evaporation from the soil, it contains more water vapor than the surrounding air.*

It lies there percolating for a time, but eventually it becomes, meteorologically speaking, *unstable*, and begins to move upward, while cooler air comes swooping in from the side. You've felt it often: The day is hot and sticky, with not a leaf stirring in the dead calm. Suddenly there is movement; leaves rustle, grass sways, and air blows across your sweaty face. "A breeze is coming up," you say. But then it dies, and the leaves grow silent, the grass still. That was no conventional breeze; that was just a thermal beginning to lift—hot air rising, and slightly less hot air blowing in to fill the void.

The warmed air lunges upward until cooler air covers the field, and then that, too, heats and eventually burps upward. Such masses of air can be visualized by thinking of a drop forming on a ceiling, expanding and hanging until suddenly it breaks free and falls.

One after another, the blobs of air (most pilots refer to them as bubbles, but that indicates a definition that probably isn't correct) rise, drifting with the wind, as weaker downdrafts sink all around. The average sink between thermals, estimates one longtime pilot, equals one fifth that of the average thermal velocity.

Now, when a gas is compressed it gets warmer, and when it expands it cools. So the blob of air, as it rises and moves into continually decreasing atmospheric pressure, expands and grows colder. The decrease in temperature is usually about 5.5 degrees F. per 1,000 feet of ascent, a decrease known as the *dry adiabatic lapse rate*. The higher the blob goes, the bigger it gets, and so the easier it is for a sailplane to stay within its confines. Some thermals, however,

---

*That's because the molecular weight of water (about 18) is less than that of dry air. All else constant, a given volume of dry air is about half again heavier than the same volume of water vapor. However, this factor is of much less importance than a difference in temperature.

may never grow larger than 100 yards across—too small for a circling glider to stay within. Others—particularly in the Plains States—go so high they measure a half mile or more across. Eventually, when the thermal reaches an altitude where the surrounding air is the same temperature, it stops, and the pilot who is up there in it must find some other area of lift.

WHAT MAKES YOU HAPPY AND WHAT DOESN'T

Thermals	*Sink*
Dark, plowed fields	Woodland
Towns	Ponds and lakes
Large factories and mills (particularly steel mills and smelting furnaces)	Slope falling away from sun
	Tidewater land
Burning dumps	Thick cropland
Gasoline tanks and refineries	Highly reflective surfaces (snow and ice)
Shopping centers	
Gravel pits and quarries	Swamps
Forest fires	
Automobile junkyards	
Large asphalt parking lots	
Rocky terrain	
Hillsides facing the sun	

(At dusk and into the night the headings are reversed. "Evening thermals" may result from warmth stored during sunlight hours in such daytime heat sinks as forests and lakes.)

This top altitude depends, of course, on the difference in temperature between the thermal and its environment—which accounts for the tall clouds seen over refinery fires, forest fires, and volcanoes. Thermals spawned as cool Canadian air blows across the hot land of the Plains States may build to 15,000 feet, and in some areas of the United States thermals have pushed sailplanes to 25,000 feet or more. Usually, however, you can expect an upper limit of perhaps 12,000 to 14,000 feet in the Western United States, usually half that in the East.

Fast-moving, high-rising thermals often occur behind cold fronts. While sun-warmed ground masses heat air from below, frigid Canadian air cools it from above, resulting in the kind of days—beginning in early morning and lasting almost to dusk—that makes sailplane pilots salivate. The ascent speed of thermals varies with the difference in temperature—according to at least one meteorological physicist, at rates ranging from less than an inch a second to more than 100 fps.

If the relative humidity in a thermal is low, or if the ascent distance is not very great, the blob eventually mixes with the rest of the air and disappears. To a sailplane pilot, that was a "blue thermal." But if the thermal is moist—if, for example, it develops after a rain or from a fresh-plowed *moist* field—then its ascent may produce a cumulus cloud, a cu. I used to lie on my back on the Caribbean island of Roatan and watch a hawk, wings outstretched, slowly spiraling upward. Then I'd sight a slanting line up along the spiral's center, and say, "A cloud should appear right *there*," and sure enough, eventually a mistiness would begin, then a hairy, wispy patch of gray, then white. Once a friend was lying next to me when I was prophesying the birth of clouds—without mentioning hawks. *That's* the way to impress.

The reason a cloud forms is that the cooling of air automatically results in an increase in the relative humidity. And when the humidity reaches 100 percent, the air no longer can hold it; the water is condensed out, changing from a gas to visible droplets. A cloud. Rising blobs of air all cool at the same rate, so all become visible at about the same altitude (the *condensation level*)—and that's the reason that clouds often look as though all their bottoms had been shaved off.

Something else happens as a cloud reaches the condensation level: It releases heat—the heat that the water absorbed earlier when the sun turned it from soil moisture to vapor—at the rate of 600 calories for every gram of water. That's a lot of heat, and it pushes the air up with increased vigor. The rising air had been cooling at the rate of 5.5 degrees per 1,000 feet, but now the cooling rate slows to 3.3 degrees per 1,000 feet, which is called, not surprisingly, the *moist* adiabatic rate. So now, as a cloud, it will rise higher, and does so at a faster rate.

If the day is very unstable, the cu may grow big and fat, feeding on itself, developing circulation of its own, sucking moist fuel from below and sending it high inside itself until the moisture grows so cold that it turns to ice crystals. Then like a huge, warped cauliflower, the cloud fans out in the classic anvil of a cumulonimbus thunderhead. Such clouds reach great heights, and some gliders have been sucked up thousands of feet in them, amid the lightning and thunder and wild turbulence. The history of soaring tells of dozens of them, dive breaks open or not. For example, back in the nineteen-thirties, Germany's Heinrich Dittmar wrote about his breaking of the international altitude record, rising 12,630 feet, mostly inside a massive cumulus cloud:

Hardly was I inside the cloud when I was greeted by the first violent gusts, and the farther I flew into it the more the machine became the plaything of the up-and-downward-moving air currents.

The variometer . . . hit the end of the scale; the speed indicator went up to 150 kilometers an hour, only to return to zero at the next moment; a frightful jolt, and I am hanging in the safety straps, but I cannot make out what position the machine has got into.

To avoid its breaking up, I try to keep the speed as low as possible, but I succeed only with great difficulty. The compass is continually turning around, the turn indicator sticks to the right, and the inclinometer also does what it likes. In addition, dirt from the skid flies up into my eyes. But the altimeter goes up and up; that is the chief thing.

A not so happy ending to another tale was described by the German science writer Leo Loebsack, in *Our Atmosphere*:

During favorable weather the Rhoen is a veritable glider's paradise, but on a close summer day in 1938 . . . a tragic misadventure occurred [when] five daring contestants flew into a thunder cloud. . . .

All five of them were suddenly sucked into the center of a violent squall. It jerked the gliders upward and the dense cloud blotted out all visibility. Fearing they would be thrown against a cliff, or perhaps because their gliders were already damaged, the flyers jumped and pulled the release cords of their parachutes.

The consequences were dreadful. Instead of falling gently downwards, the parachutes were filled to bursting point by the wind and carried upwards. Higher and higher they soared into increasingly colder layers of the cloud. However hard they tried to steer with their arms and legs, they could not escape the howling force of the gale. Huge raindrops soaked their bodies in a few seconds. Hailstones lashed their faces. . . .

We do not know all that happened between earth and sky during these frightful minutes, as only one man, severely injured, escaped with his life. We can only imagine the ordeal of the other four. At a height of thirty-five, forty-five or even fifty thousand feet, they must have been enclosed in a casing of frozen water, tossed about like living icicles, stabbed at by lightning, until the cloud released their four lifeless bodies.

Most of the time, of course, such thermal-produced clouds remain small, with short lives. Just as the top of a cloud has reached mature formation, the bottom ordinarily has already turned wispy—like hair that has begun to be undone —and the formerly strong thermal beneath the cloud has pulled itself up inside. And then through evaporation, the cloud decays, having had a visible life cycle of only about 15 to 30 minutes. The sky may continually be dotted with clouds, but each is in a process of growth or decay, and in a half hour none of the original may be left.

One of the judgments that a good sailplane pilot develops is a sense of what part of its life a cloud is going through. Look, say the experts, for clouds that are well defined, that have sharp edges, that are round and firm and crisp and fresh and advancing toward middle-age spread. Look, too, for a cu with a concave base, indicative of entering air. And watch (through Polaroid sunglasses) for hazy wisps that mark the beginning of a new cloud.

That's what they say. But beginners cannot understand the language; they go rushing off to the nearest likely cloud only to see it vanish into a column of sink. They must get up there, to understand, up under the cu, and look at it, decide what it's doing, then see if it does what it's supposed to. They must do that again and again and again, and eventually predictive power will improve. But it's a slow process.

One of the worst times for thermals are days with *inversions*, days in which instead of the air steadily growing cooler with height, a warm layer overlays the area. That's *stable* air, and it's not to be desired. The hot layer is a ceiling through which no thermal can rise, and the few thermals that form below it remain weak and thin. Often such a day is hazy, and if you fly up in a power craft you can see the inversion layer as a thin leer of haze—the accumulated pollen, dust, and assorted pollution held captive below the inversion.

But on wonderfully thermic days, one cloud may be followed by others cooking loose from particularly healthy sources. Assembled by the wind, the result might be cumulus clouds stretched out in what is called a cloud street, "lined up like conveniently located service stations," reported one national champion after a winning day. "I jumped from one to another all afternoon long." Get on the right cloud street and you don't even have to circle: Simply fly at your lowest sink rate in the thermals, and between, get the nose down and hold it there until the variometer begins to bob up again.

Now back to what thermals look like, or at least what the soaring pilot can visualize them as. Most pilots think of them as ice-cream cones, leaning with the wind, not straight but a little wobbly, something like a tornado. The mental picture can be refined by thinking of the cone as consisting of a string of huge, rising blobs. Between the blobs, air usually continues to rise in a sort of chimney effect, but at a much reduced rate. That's the reason that one plane might be rising at a healthy clip while one directly above and another below are barely holding their own. If cus are forming, check their size, and by extending lines down to, perhaps, a parking-lot-size patch on the ground, you might be able to get some idea of the cone's approximate dimensions.

The contours of the rising blobs were first more or less defined by British meteorologist R. S. Scorer in the mid-fifties. Others had released large containers of warm smoke into the atmosphere in order to see what a thermal might really look like, but none of the attempts were truly successful. Scorer attacked it from another direction. He released various-size, white-colored masses of heavy liquid into a large, glass tank, then filmed the result. No matter the size, all of the bubbles exhibited a common characteristic: a doughnut shape, turning inside out as they sunk.

Flip the whole demonstration over, change the substances from liquid to gas, and you probably have a fairly accurate representation of a thermal, says Scorer. It's an invisible smoke ring, called a vortex shell. The central core rises rapidly, but the outer edge rises hardly at all, or perhaps even moves downward (one reason why a sailplane often encounters high sink just before entering a thermal).

Much of the time the thermal probably looks less like a doughnut than like a section of a steep-sided funnel. What happens, then, when a sailplane centers in a large thermal is that it rises rapidly through that vortex—considerably faster than the thermal is rising—and when it reaches a point somewhere near the top, the rate of climb diminishes until it is rising at the same rate of speed as the warm air blob as a whole. Something like a Ping-Pong ball bobbing atop a rising fountain.

The concept also explains why an uncentered sailplane tends easily to lose the thermal; it is literally flung off of the top into sink. And that's why (at low altitudes, especially) thermals are a lot easier to locate than to stay in—in fact, the ease with which they are found surprises most beginning sailplane pilots. It's staying in them that separates the eagles from the magpies.

The technique for best finding thermals and keeping them (as is the best way of doing almost anything in soaring) can cause heavy discussion in the pilots' lounge. Here, however, is a compendium of procedures, a collection of techniques melded into a single guideline to find thermals and, once found, to hold them:

1. Start looking upwind of the field, so you'll have more time before you're out of altitude.

2. Select a point in the distance and aim for it, adjusting your speed for the best L/D speed (in an 1-26, for example, about 45 mph, which produces a sink rate of about 3.3 fps) to cover a lot of territory economically. (Or, if you have a MacCready ring, use that to find the best speed to fly, once you've risen in a thermal or two.) Beginners often believe they should fly at the lowest sink rate (in the 1-26, 38 mph, which gives a 2.6 fps sink). This is faulty thinking. Even though the plane might be sinking more slowly, it takes so much more time to reach the destination that you arrive at a significantly lower altitude. If you encounter areas of heavier than normal sink, go even faster.

3. Fly absolutely straight and level, so you can feel every little twitch of the craft. With sloppy flying you don't know if those twitches are rising packets of air or your own lack of coordination.

4. Don't allow those bumps to deviate your flight path. If a thermal lifts one of your wings and you let the plane enter even a slight induced roll, it will turn a bit—right out of the thermal. On the other hand, don't make automatic corrections without realizing that you're correcting.

5. If you are high (3,000 feet or more), you can be selective. Don't grab the first puff you find; try for something with substance to it. If you are low, of course, take whatever you can get; it might be your last chance.

6. Pay attention to three things simultaneously: (a) your flying and other aircraft, (b) jiggles of the plane, and (c) the variometer.

7. If you're flying smoothly, chances are you'll *feel* rising air before you see it on the variometer. As soon as you feel your wing wiggle, watch the variometer closely; when it flutters upward, you either react immediately or you don't—depending on which expert's advice you're following.

(a) Some say turn *instantly* toward the rising wing, the stronger the twitch the sharper the turn, averaging, perhaps, a 35-degree bank. They say that 90 percent of the time the glider is whisking across only the outer fringes of a thermal, and if the pilot waits until he gets a solid reading on his variometer, he'll lose the lift and probably never find it again.

(b) Most of the rest of the experts recommend counting to three (or five), *then* making the turn.

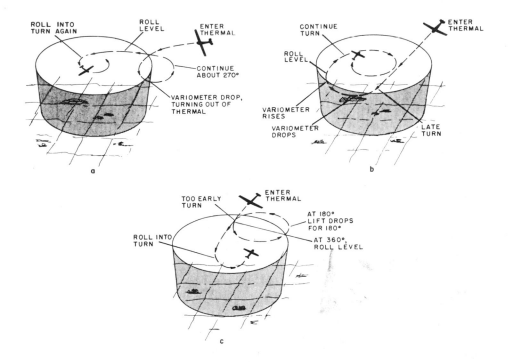

Centering from (a) a turn in the wrong direction, (b) a turn too late, and (c) a turn too early.

(c) And a few say do nothing at all. Simply count and wait to see which wing is lifting. Then when the variometer has dramatically *dropped*, whip the plane around in the direction of the lifted wing, and count again until you've gone through about three quarters of the numbers (if you counted to eight, now count to six), then turn sharply into the lift to begin steep, slow-speed circling.

Best advice: Try all three, then modify until eventually you settle on whatever works for you.

8. At any rate, once you bank into what looks like a thermal, slow to the best sink speed for the bank angle, and watch your variometer to see what it does: consistently up, and you're into the thermal; an immediate down, of course, and you're not. In either case, complete the turn at a constant, well-coordinated speed and angle of bank. Changes in bank or speed, as well as slipping and skidding, can warp the circle into an ellipse, and the eventual result: out of the thermal. And unless a total-energy system (a sophisticated, lift-indicating instrument) is used, sloppy flying will give indications of lift where none exists.

At any rate, if you find no lift, go around once more. Still none? Some instructors say try a quick turn in the opposite direction. Others say that's a waste of time; give up and head again toward your original reference point.

9. But the likelihood is that you will find lift, and now your problem is centering. Again, different schools:

(a) The "lower-wing rule" states that when you're trying to center in a thermal, at the point of lowest lift (or greatest sink) the plane's lower wing is pointing directly at the thermal's core. Continue your turn another 90 degrees, flatten your bank a bit (changing the circle to an oval) to move yourself over, then resume circling. Don't try to move over too far or you might pop out of the thermal's other side.

(b) If there's an immediate cessation of lift at the beginning of the turn, chances are you turned the wrong way, out of the thermal. Continue around about 270 degrees, roll level, count to three, and roll into the same turn again; see (a) in diagram on facing page.

(c) A late turn is indicated by disappearance of lift at about the 90-degree point. Continue turning until the variometer starts to rise again, then quickly roll out, wait a moment or two, then roll in again.

(d) A too-early turn is indicated by good lift for 180 degrees, and poor or none for 180 degrees; see (c). Complete a full 360-degree turn, roll out, count, roll back. When your variometer needle stays put all the way around, of course, you've found the core.

Don't try to remember the steps. Simply trace them, looking at the diagrams, until they make sense. You might even close your eyes and visualize thermaling sequences. Or better, when you're sitting around waiting for the day's thermals to build, on a pad of paper draw some circles (thermals from the top) and figure out what you should do when entering them from different angles. What you *don't* want to do is memorize rules; aim to understand thermals so well that your logic will see you through.

If you join somebody else in a thermal, you must circle in the same direction as he; in fact, if a dozen of you are in a single thermal (not all that rare during competitions)—called a "gaggle" of sailplanes—all must turn in the same direction. If you don't, you'll lose friends. In fact, even the *birds* will be unhappy, as Central America pilot Clarence Crawford noted in a letter published in *Soaring*:

I was instructing over the Panama Canal Zone [when] I spotted a large circle of hawks and buzzards climbing in a right-hand spiral about a mile away and called this to the attention of my student, Jack Davis. As we started gliding toward them, I turned the controls over to him while I began making routine entries in the log book. Suddenly there was an awful squawking. We were in the middle of the birds. They were flying in disarray in all directions, scolding, and even making simulated attacks on us.
"What's happening?" I asked Jack.
"Aw, they're just sore because I came into their thermal circling left when they were circling right," he explained.
"Well, get us out of this mess," I ordered. "Then come back in the thermal the proper way."
He did as I told him. Would you believe it?—when we reentered the thermal, this time carefully spiraling in the same direction, there was no more clamor. The birds seemed to look at us as if to say, "Your manners have improved. *Now* you're doing it right!"

WAVES

If, in a smooth-flowing brook, you lay a water-soaked log so that it rests crosswise a few inches below the surface, the water will lift to pass over it, then sharply dip, then rise again perhaps a foot downstream, dip again, lift again, and so on until the undulations no longer can be seen.

Substitute for that log a mountain or mountain range or large plateau, and for the water, air. Each ripple becomes a *lee wave* or *mountain wave* or *standing wave*—or simply a *wave*—and it's one of the best things ever to have happened to sailplane pilots.

Waves first were recognized in the lee of Czechoslovakia's Sudeten Mountains in the late thirties. In the United States, they were found in 1940,

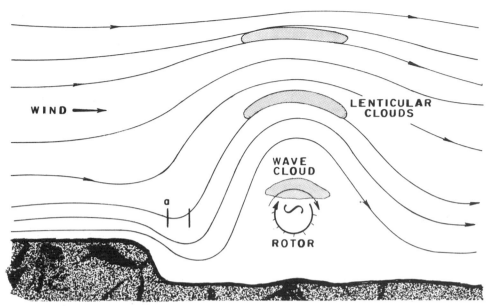

WIND ⟶

LENTICULAR CLOUDS

WAVE CLOUD

ROTOR

A wave is formed as air moves swiftly across mountains or drops off a plateau, then rebounds upward. Other sets of clouds may appear downwind.

when John Robinson soared over Sun Valley, Idaho. Soon it was discovered that other Western areas, particularly downwind of the Sierra Nevadas, were even better. Waves needed huge mountains, everyone thought, and American waves were purely Western events. Whenever they could, pilots would go trekking off to Bishop, California, sailplane Mecca.

Now, suddenly, in just the last few years, soaring pilots are looking for waves in the East—and they're finding them all along the Allegheny Mountains—all along the whole Appalachians, in fact, from Maine to Georgia. Today Pennsylvania is known as the best long-distance launch pad in the world, and both the men's and women's world long-distance records were set there (see next chapter), the pilots sailing ridge lift, thermals, and finally waves from the middle of Pennsylvania to the far edge of Virginia and beyond.

Further, waves are not limited to what is ordinarily thought of as mountain states. Weather satellites have now detected waves in all states but a handful—only a few in the Deep South, and a few more in a small circle of heartland centered on Wisconsin.

Just a few days ago, in the last week of April, I got another taste of Allegheny wave soaring, an event that a decade ago would have been notable. Now it's commonplace: Anyone can duplicate it a dozen times or more a year.

I walked out onto the field about noon with little hope of finding anything in the sky. It was heavily overcast, promising to begin another typical Pennsylvania drizzler—irritating, chilly, depressing. But when I looked to the northwest, there was a sight that made me forget all about my ill mood: Stretched across the slush-colored clouds like a giant wound in the sky was a slash of dazzling blue rimmed with cloud banks piled like folded-back sheets. That was a wave, or, rather, the dip before the wave.

Towed to 3,000 feet and released below that opening, I saw that even in closeup the gash looked like a huge roll of cotton batting slit with a scalpel. And down below, a world of gloom was divided neatly in half by a line of sunlight dashes running perpendicular to the wind—proof that what I was aiming for was indeed a wave.

I started the flight by sinking at nearly 400 fpm. I had misjudged. Stuck in the downflow. But then, suddenly, I wasn't dropping at all: I bottomed out, then began lifting, caught in the upwelling wave, coasting upward, the variometer now having shifted its needle to *plus* 400, and I was rising, rising up right into that grinning gash.

And then it started to close. Both ends seemed to zip together, until only a center rectangle remained. One day in 1969, as an observer in a heavily instrumented Department of Commerce DC-6, I flew at 6,000 feet eleven times through the eye of hurricane Laurie. Now I was reminded of that eye in miniature—vertical walls, seething clouds of dirty fluff, searing-blue sky above, and murk below. And, I must admit, I was a bit apprehensive—partly because the hole threatened to snap shut around me, but mostly because if it began to close, I'd immediately have to drop. And I didn't want to.

Ordinarily, in such a situation I wouldn't have gone through that opening at all, wouldn't have gambled against the possibility that I'd be caught atop the clouds. (A slug of moisture-laden air could have blown down from Lake Erie to plug that opening.) But I knew what waves usually do in this area, and all signs pointed toward the probability that the rent in the sky would stay there—in one size or another—all day. And if it were to close, similar openings would be nearby.

And sure enough, I wound back and forth in the chimney (it couldn't have been more than 400 feet across), S-curving gradually upward, finally to enter the breathtaking sunshine found only on the tops of clouds, and I saw scattered off in the distance a dozen similar windows slowly zipping open and closed.

I was able to rise no higher than 5,900 feet that day, and that was okay; I had no place to go anyway. (And it *was* higher than the Louisiana altitude record.) For the next couple of hours I simply cruised along the southeast flank in air so eerily smooth I could have been watching a wraparound movie. When finally, reluctantly, I decided to go back down, the air masses seemed equally reluctant to let me, so strong were they streaming upward.

The flight that day was hardly extraordinary. My top altitude barely topped a mile (some Appalachian pilots have risen nearly five); I strayed no more than a half dozen miles from the airport; I had not a whit of trouble staying up. Yet the flight was awesome—as soaring in waves always seems to be. Thermals and ridge lift you can sort out in your head; you can get a handle on what the wind is doing, what the lifting force must be, what the dimensions of the components are. Both of them seem familiar—back-yard phenomena. But a *wave*! You get up there in all that smooth, subtle understatedness and you can't help but be humbled by the *immensity* of it all, the enormity of the machinery. The *power*.

A wave is a giant meteorological machine, and the one I was in worked something like this: Some three miles west-northwest of me the Allegheny Plateau stretches northeast to southwest. If the wind is blowing from about 310 degrees (give or take about 30 degrees) and is constant, and if the wind speed gradually, smoothly increases with altitude, then the air makes a mammoth waterfall. It plunges over the 1,200-foot-high plateau in a layer thousands of feet thick, and bounces; the weight of all that air falling over the precipice compresses the air below it, and it actually rebounds. It reaches a great height, then falls again, bounces once more, and again and again—resonating off across central Pennsylvania like those ripples in the brook.

Such variations can cause three kinds of clouds:

Rotor, a rolling, tubular cloud, wispy and straggly, seemingly in slow-motion turmoil as it continuously forms and tears itself apart, flinging out strags of tortured substance in the process. Scattered strings of these *fracto cumulus* rotors often appear and disappear, materializing and dissipating, along a stretch perpendicular to the wind—in the Appalachians, only 1,500 to about 2,000 feet above the land. They're more or less made up of local air tumbled by the wind whipping up and over them. If sufficiently dense, they're called "roll clouds."

Wave cloud, resting atop or raised above the rotor at 2,500 to 4,500 feet (in the East) above the landscape, with a typical thickness of 1,500 feet or so. Sometimes the wave cloud looks like a continuation of the rotor, except more substantial, more cumuluslike. This cloud too is continually forming and dissipating—becoming visible on the upwind side as rising air reaches the condensation level, then cresting up and over to disappear again as the wind loses altitude. Often the cloud is relatively thick on the leading edge, thin on the trailing, like a wing.

Lenticular cloud—high, thin, almond- or airfoil-shaped—the only cloud that many pilots associate with waves. It typically appears at 20,000 to 30,000

Some 9,000 feet above the Owens Valley, on the eastern side of the Sierra Nevada, a standing rotor cloud writhes (upper left) as dust streaks on the valley floor. (Courtesy of Mrs. Robert Symons, Bishop, CA)

feet, and is much less substantial than it seems from the ground. Usually, if you are lucky enough to fly up near one, this hard-edged, lens-shaped cloud grows thinner as you get closer, so that when you finally approach it, it disappears altogether.

If the high-altitude air holds little moisture, the lenticular cloud fails to appear, and if lower-level air isn't sufficiently humid, no clouds at all will be seen—and then finding the correct spot to soar into a wave becomes simply a combination of experience and luck.

One remarkable thing about all of these clouds—rotor, wave, and lenticular—is that even when the wind is blowing through them at near-gale force, they stay emplaced, forming at the front, dissipating at the rear.

Or the opposite. Often the evidence of a wave appears not as a cloud that is forming, but as one disappearing—the situation on the day of my April flight. The air warmed as it descended, was able to hold more water, so the cloud disappeared ("evaporated"), then reappeared again as the air bounced upward past the condensation level. That was the window I climbed through, elevating upward far on the front side of the rotor, then sailing along in the quiet of the rising wave-cloud wind.

In the West, of course, with its towering mountain ranges and half-mile-deep canyons, if you don't require oxygen in a wave, the trip hardly seems worth the bother. There, the harmonic wave motions may continue for hundreds of miles rollercoastering eastward—lift before the crests, sink before the troughs. Vertical currents of 1,000 fpm are common, lift of 3,000 fpm is seen occasionally, and there are reports of rare upwellings nearly double that. The waves go high, too; it was in a wave over the Mojave Desert that the world altitude record was set by Paul Bikle back in 1961, when he soared from 3,964 feet to 46,267, higher than commercial jets can fly. He used oxygen, but no pressurization. The record is limited, says the Soaring Society of America, "only by physiological constraints."

OTHER TYPES OF SOARABLE LIFT

Ridge, thermal, and wave are by far the most widespread kinds of usable lift, but others are occasionally available. Some of them:

Shear or Convergence Lift
When two masses of air come together, there's nowhere for them to go but up, and if a sailplane is at the convergence zone, it too may rise. The trouble is, a mild meeting gives little lift, whereas a strong frontal convergence—a cold front underrunning a warm mass, for instance—will produce not only strong shear lift and probably thermals, but also squalls, thunderstorms, violent turbulence. Beware.

Sea Breeze
On sunny days, the land along a shoreline heats much faster than the water offshore, warming the air lying atop it. The warmed air begins to rise, and the cool, dense air over the

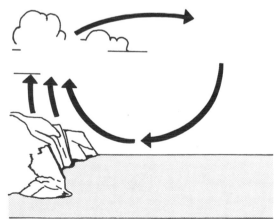

Sea-breeze lift.

water flows in to fill the space—whereupon it is heated and rises, sometimes producing a line of clouds along the shore. That first American long-distance glide, the 1928 flight by Peter Hasselbach, was on a shoreside sea breeze at Cape Cod. If the general air mass is moving toward the water, then a *sea-breeze front* may develop, an accented sea-breeze condition.

Dust Devil

This is a particularly intense thermal, so strong that it picks up debris from the earth, and so reveals its outline. It begins with a slight rotation of rising air; other air rushes in, and the converging masses begin rotating even more strongly as the whirlwind circumference reduces—something like a spinning ice skater speeding up by folding his arms to his body. Dust devils can sometimes be seen as high as 5,000 feet, and probably rise well above that. They are not "mild tornadoes." They begin on the heated surface, while tornadoes are triggered by cooling aloft; and dust devils are dry, tornadoes wet. Can be a little rough, but usually are safe to soar in.

Horizontal Cylindrical Roll

This is a rare beast. It requires a large valley with a mountain sitting in its middle. Wind blows down the valley, separates to flow around the mount, then converges again, and if conditions are right, rolls away in a huge double helix. In California's Tehachapi Valley, for example, pilots soar back and forth atop the roll several thousand feet high for about five miles.

Meteorologists admit that they are often confused by waves, and when they try to predict them, more than occasionally fail. The mechanism is extraordinarily complicated, and the number of factors that must be pumped into the formula is staggering. For example, the size of the mountain range doesn't always indicate the size of the wave. What's more important is the *resonance* of the wavelength, which is a function of the temperature gradient, the wind speed and direction at various levels, and even of the *width* of the range. Best advice if you're in a wave area: On fall, winter, and early spring days when the wind seems to be coming briskly from the right direction (no more than 30 degrees off perpendicular to the range or plateau) behind a cold front or just before a warm front, check the sky one to three hours after sunrise or before sunset, usually the best times.

Enter the wave lift not through the rotor, but well upwind, if possible, and as soon as you feel the silky smoothness of true wave lift, turn into the wind. Then slow to minimum sink and, ideally, determine what speed to fly to maintain position over a spot on the ground. You do that by finding an easily seen landmark—a house, for example—and holding the mark still as you sight it through the canopy. As you rise, you might also slowly edge forward, because at high altitudes you usually find that your best rate of climb is upwind of the starting position.

Flying with others is especially helpful here. If someone drifts back or penetrates too far, he can always spot the others, marking the place. You may have to speed up a little to guard against being blown up and back, over the hump (almost like maintaining upwind position before a ridge). And you may also have to run serial S-turns, or back-and-forth tacks, crabbing to match wind velocity, so you won't glide too far upwind. At any rate, turn *into* the wind, avoiding 360-degree turns—again, as though you were working ridge lift—because an accidental swoop into the rotor can mean real trouble.

A rotor ride is one of the three dangers associated with wave soaring. The first is that the sky will close up, trapping you up there, disoriented, out of visual touch with the ground with no choice but to drop down through the clouds.

The second is that you'll get so enchanted with the pursuit of altitude that you won't realize that you're becoming oxygen starved, suffering from hypoxia. You get up above 15,000 feet or so and you'll probably find an insidious intoxication coming on, coupled with a high degree of self-confidence, almost euphoria, sleepiness, and miscoordination. And the big trouble is that you probably won't even notice. Deadly. Most authorities recommend using oxygen above 12,500 feet. If you smoke, better cut that to 10,000.

And the rotor: In the East, probably the worst thing that could happen in a rotor is that you'd be bumped around, maybe smacking your head on the canopy. (Good idea to stuff a pair of socks into your hat if you expect high turbulence.) But in the West, rotors can be incredibly violent, and experienced pilots avoid them at all costs.

The story of Larry Edgar's April 25, 1955, flight will show why. He had been flying since midmorning in a Pratt-Read, riding the Sierra Wave and reaching a maximum altitude of just under 40,000 feet. The temperature was frigid—more than –60 degrees F, but Edgar was dressed for it. Only his feet were a little chilly.

About 2 P.M. he radioed the airport in Bishop, California, that he was coming down. Then he saw little tufts of churning cloud out ahead of the main roll cloud. He increased his speed to penetrate into the strong wind—

My flight path went into the very top of the little cloud as it seemed to swell up before me at the last moment. I looked at the needle and ball. Suddenly and instantaneously the needle went off center about two thirds of the way. I followed with correction, but before I reached the neutral position, the needle violently swung the other way. Shearing action was terrific. I was forced sideways in my seat, first to the left, then to the right. At the same time the shearing force threw me to the right, a fantastic positive G load shoved me down into the seat—my head went forward and my chin was pressed hard against my chest. I could feel my body crumple in the seat as I blacked out. Then a violent roll to the left with a loud explosion was instantaneously followed with a crushing negative G load.

I was unable to see after blacking out, but I was conscious and felt my head hit the canopy with the negative load. There was a lot of noise, and I was taking quite a beating at this time. . . .

Then, just as suddenly as all this violence had started, it became quiet, except for the sound of the wind whistling by. I felt that I had been thrown clear of the glider. There was no sensation of falling, but rather one of being suspended out in space.

Something was holding both my feet. I tried to move them, but it had a firm grip. I tried to look at my feet and see what was holding them, but I still couldn't see; everything was black.

There seemed to be no twisting, shaking or tumbling in the fall. However, I must admit I was very much confused. I was still trying to squirm and pull my feet free, but I couldn't do it. I fell a way and then decided it best to try to open the parachute anyway. I felt and fumbled across my chest until I found the ripcord. I yanked; the parachute opened immediately—what a wonderful feeling!

At the same instant both my feet were free. My boots went when the parachute slammed open, so I was in my socks. Everything was black. It was quiet. All of this violence had taken place in just a few seconds. Now, for the first time I could really keep up with what was going on. If I could only see! My helmet, gloves, and oxygen mask were all gone. My feet were cool even though I had on three pairs of socks. The slippers went off with the boots. . . .

[Suddenly] vision in my right eye returned—it was blurred but so helpful. The first thing I saw was a faint light moving very slowly back and forth. It took me a moment to figure out this was the sun. I was in cloud, but it was not dense enough to completely blank out the sun.

I looked up at the parachute. It was a colorful thing, with orange and white panels. There were some broken shroud lines. I looked down and noticed the ground through a little hole in the cloud. Now I realized what made the sun appear to move back and forth. I was turning and swinging on the parachute quite violently at times. Now and then the parachute would suddenly yank me upward.

I came out just below the main roll-cloud. It was a massive, dark, boiling thing. I didn't want to be carried upward so I pulled on the shrouds on one side to partially collapse the parachute. For the first time, free of the cloud, I could see parts of the Pratt-Read being carried upward past me. This was the first I had seen of the glider since hitting the turbulence, and it was my first indication that 195 had broken up in the air. I had not been thrown out because of a loose belt.

Seeing pieces of fabric and plywood going up and disappearing in the roll-cloud was quite an impressive sight, and I cannot express my feelings as I swung there on the parachute and realized these were pieces of 195. It may sound funny to some and inadequate to others, but at that time I exclaimed aloud, "Darn!" . . .

The shroud lines pulled my left wrist in front of the left eye, so my wristwatch was right in front of my right eye. I wasn't particularly interested in the time, but since that was the thing I saw, I noticed the watch said ten minutes after three.

My right hand was bleeding profusely. Vision in my left eye was still gone, and I was concerned with having lost it as the left side of my face was all wet.

The wind was carrying me eastward over the valley. I was three or four miles south of Bishop. It looked as though I might land on the White Mountains to the east. I still couldn't tell that I was doing very well with the problem of getting down. I kept on tugging at the shrouds, which was very exhausting. Then, gradually, the roll-cloud began to look a little higher and I could tell by the crest of the mountains that I was coming down.

I looked at my watch. . . . Ten minutes had gone by since I first looked at it. My right arm was becoming very tired of holding the shroud lines, but now I could see with my left eye! It was not possible to focus it, but I could see. I found it better to keep it shut and try to look with just the right eye.

I heard the BT towplane engine, and I was hoping they would see me. Al Langenheim did see me, reported my position to Bishop and flew around me. . . .

I was drifting backward . . . quite rapidly, perhaps twenty or twenty-five miles per hour. I felt I should try to turn around by grasping across the shroud lines, but still I could not raise my left arm high enough to accomplish this. I did grasp the fittings to disconnect the harness from the parachute, but I failed to act fast enough. I was stunned by the landing and do not recall being dragged on my face through the gravel.

Pieces of Edgar's sailplane—one of the strongest models ever built—were gathered and analyzed, and the sequence of events and forces required to demolish it were eventually determined. Control cables had been yanked apart, the tail boom and one wing had been ripped off, and the nose had been plucked away from the body. The force required to accomplish this was 16 Gs, and more than 10,000 pounds.

Larry Edgar recovered completely.

Chapter Nine

Cross-Country Flight: Putting It All Together

Cross-country record breakers are a special breed. They get up hours before dawn. They wrap themselves in so many layers of clothing they resemble artichokes. Wedged into coffin-size cockpits, they half-sit, half-lie, barely moving in deepfreeze for five, eight, ten hours—all the time knocked and slammed and buffeted by weather guaranteed to be cantankerous. And as often as not, far from their goal, they drop unappreciated into some farmer's field, eventually to suffer the ignominy of telephoning someone to come and get them. Back at their home field again, they immediately start thinking about the next attempt, for they are single-minded, driven, obsessed.

They're also rare—or at least the good ones are. Sunday sailplane pilots rarely get out of gliding range of the airport. On fair days they'll stay within three or four miles of the field, playing with the thermals, riding the ridge. And

Cross-country pilot, going for distance, gets ready to take off at dawn.

on good days, when they are carried up to 6,000 or 7,000 feet, they'll venture perhaps a dozen miles away, secure in the knowledge that they can still make it back to the runway in a single long glide.

For those who are in the sport strictly for the relaxation—for the instant therapy that soaring can bring—local flying is sublime; it's all they need. But some pilots demand a challenge. They like to test themselves as they strive to gather points for increasingly difficult SSA awards (see box)—and that means venturing away from the field, called "leaving the nest" the first time it's done.

FOR COMPETITORS

Soaring offers three kinds of competition. The first is the attempt to gain records—distance, speed, height. (See Appendix for current holders.)

The second kind of competition takes the form of assigned *tasks*, cross-country flights around a course for speed. As *Soaring* columnist George Moffat once pointed out, such contests develop personalities of their own: "Some are cutthroat affairs you can cut with a knife. Some are so 'just-folks' that flying is an afterthought."

"As a spectator sport," adds competition pilot Grenville Seibels, "it is a poor second to chess-by-mail. Everyone dives across the start line at an altitude of one kilometer, disappears for three to five hours, then, if all goes well, returns to land. Big deal." But then he adds, "I realize, after all, that there is no other sport worthy of my serious attention." It's also one of the few sports in which you can hope to compete in the nationals within a year or two of first getting interested.

The third kind of competition is the pilot vying with himself—according to the SSA, because (as is stated in its excellent *Soaring Flight Manual*) "every flight should have some particular goal in mind, since nothing leads to boredom faster than flying aimlessly around an airport at the top of a thermal. Boredom leads to the development of bad or careless habits." The rules, developed by the international FAI and overseen by the SSA, set a series of tasks that grow progressively difficult. The scheme involves entrapment: The first ones are so easy (you get your A badge after solo, a B for "proficiency," a C when you are ready for cross-country) that you're surprised when you are handed a pin. And then you're pleased when, after you've done a one-hour flight, your name appears in *Soaring*, along with your C badge number. (Some 11,000 pilots had been numbered by mid-1981, and they're increasing by about 500 a year.)

After the A, B, and C badges come the silver and gold badges, and then diamonds on the gold badge. Top badge is a gold with three diamonds, one jewel each for:

- A flight of at least 300 kilometers over a triangular or out-and-return course.
- A distance flight of 500 kilometers (311 statute miles).
- A height gain of 5,000 meters (16,400 feet). In the half century that badges have been around, fewer than 2,000 pilots in the whole world have earned all three, scarcely 500 of them in the United States.

Stan Smith prepares his AS-W 15 at the 1980 nationals at Harris Hill, New York. He also flew in the first United States meet at Harris Hill, fifty years before.

That first time is unforgettable. *Every* time is exhilarating, but that first time takes real courage. Leaving the comfort of known winds and thermals, and getting *out of sight* of the home field requires a mixture of confidence and adrenaline that takes some time to accumulate. It requires a thorough understanding of moving air masses; it requires use of all those basic techniques of flying that the pilot has been trying to perfect; and it requires self-assurance. Fortunately, the idea of an off-field landing is so unnerving to a new pilot that by the time he has developed his courage, he has probably also developed his ability. Few try cross-country flying before they are able. And unlike most other sports, soaring allows the participant to determine his own level of risk.

Among those who do practice cross-country, only a small fraction are really good at it. And a superior *woman* cross-country pilot is rarer still. Of the 16,000 members of SSA, only a few hundred pilots participate in competition, and of the 200 to 300 active women soaring pilots, not many more than a dozen compete.

One who does is Doris Grove, mother of six, gentle and kind and feminine and maternal. But somewhere hidden beneath that mild exterior is a volcano of determination, stamina, drive.

Doris Grove tries for records. In November 1980 she made a 300-kilometer out-and-return (O & R) flight in a 15-meter plane at an average speed of 71 mph, and so became the first woman to hold any national record in a *general* category (still pending as this is written), as opposed to the women's category. She holds so many state records they're hard to keep track of. And she was the first woman ever to soar for more than 1,000 kilometers (1,000.868 k, or 621.4 miles) all in one swoop.

To illustrate how all of the soaring techniques fit together—the theory, the stick-and-rudder skill, the judgment, the sensitivity to the atmosphere—here is the story of that 1,000-kilometer flight, a story that was unique in that it was a first, but otherwise, typical of O&R attempts, and useful as a template.

The flight took place on March 11, 1980, but the preparation started the previous fall, when Canadian cold fronts began that year's annual cold-weather march across the Alleghenies. Brisk, sustained northwest winds mean ridge lift on the Pennsylvania mountain slopes, and probably waves as well, and every dedicated sailplane pilot in the region watches the evening weather report to plot the progress of the fronts. "From November to April I check the weather day and night," says Doris. "I keep track of how many hours of daylight there are too. And I can't tell you how many times that winter I got up at three or four o'clock to call Flight Service" (the Federal Aviation Administration agency that provides pilots with weather data).

Her goal was simple: to be the first woman ever to soar 1,000 kilometers. Her plan was to take off early in the morning and follow the Alleghenies from

A.J. Smith, 1968 world champion in the Standard Class (contest held at Leszno, Poland), tapes the joints of his Hornet to eliminate as much drag as possible.)

Sailplanes line up for takeoff at the fiftieth anniversary of the first national soaring contest, Harris Hill, New York.

Laszlo Horvath snaps twin cameras into their holders as he prepares his AS-W 20 for the day's task during the 1980 nationals.

Julian, Pennsylvania (where she is half owner of Ridge Soaring Gliderport), past Altoona, over a snip of Maryland at Cumberland, then south-southwest along the Virginia–West Virginia border to Bluefield, West Virginia, just forty-five miles from the Tennessee line. Then turn around and come back. And it wasn't just getting there and back; it was doing it *fast*—because the days of winter allow few hours to dawdle.

Most of the time Doris would ride ridge lift. But she would also have to use thermals or waves to carry her across the half dozen gaps. Her plane, a Schleicher AS-W 19, is exquisite, but it's not the optimum. It's a *standard*-class sailplane, and most distance records are won in *open*-class ships—which simply means higher performance, mainly because the wings are longer (20 meters or more, as compared with 15), which, in turn, means a few more critical L/D points.

Four times that winter she had already tried it. The first time, she landed at Keyser, West Virginia, in a field smooth enough that a towplane could come for her. The second time she made it almost to Cumberland, Maryland, but then she ran into rain. The lift disappeared, so she turned back and landed at the Bedford, Pennsylvania, airport—again to be aerotowed back home.

The third time she whizzed well past Bedford, making fine time, when suddenly the bottom dropped out; a wave happened to be so placed that downflow struck the ridge, suppressing lift. Again she had to land. This time a friend drove down to retrieve her by car.

Now was the night of March 10, a rainy, blustery, nor'westerly night, the kind of night that makes forecasters apologize, but makes ridge runners cancel the next day's appointments. Wild northwest rain was a good sign. A better sign was that the six-o'clock TV weather show from Penn State showed that a high-pressure center was moving down from the west, that the pressure gradient was tight, and that a front was pushing through. (One study of 153 long, cross-country flights shows that four out of five of them were made after a cold front had passed and before the following high-pressure center arrived.)

But the best sign appeared at three-thirty-five in the morning, when Doris looked out of her window. And why was she up so late? She wasn't; she was getting up. During the ridge season she goes to bed at 8 P.M., and on days when fronts are expected to move through on high winds, she wakes up, she says, because her anxiety alarm rings. "I looked out of the bedroom window and the sky was clear, except for puffy clouds whipping in from the right direction, northwest. Usually I call Flight Service, and usually I listen to the weather-alert radio [a UHF receiver tuned to National Weather Service stations]. But this morning I didn't even bother—just came out to the field because I *knew* that this was a 1,000-kilometer day."

With her was her fifteen-year-old daughter, Rosalie, to run the wing and

Tom Knauff readies Doris Grove's AS-W 19 for an assault on the women's out-and-return record. Here he fills the water-ballast tanks.

to act as the "official observer," a person designated to see that everything is done legally. Rosalie should have been in school, but it's not every day that a girl's mother tries to break a world's record.

At four-thirty, they arrived at the field. The wind, whistling around the hangar, blew bits of dirt and leaves through the automobile headlights reflecting from the runway, still wet from the two-day rain. Rosalie and Tom Knauff, Doris's partner in Ridge Soaring (and himself holder of the world O&R record for multiplace plane: 516 miles), rolled out the AS-W 19 while Doris consulted her checklist. Tom filled the wings with a mixture of water and antifreeze, while the wind, roaring down the field, splashed it all over his arms (and there are few things colder than evaporating antifreeze), driving him into the pilots' lounge to stand before the woodstove.

The AS-W 19 holds 23 gallons (158 pounds) of water-antifreeze ballast that performs two functions: increases the gross weight so that the plane can *penetrate* better, can drive quickly through a headwind, and it stabilizes the wings, allowing them to absorb turbulence shocks instead of passing them on to the pilot.

While Tom readied the plane, Doris changed into her flying gear: snow-mobile suit over two wool sweaters over two pairs of long johns. And on each foot: (1) two men's wool socks, (2) a felt liner, (3) a sheepskin liner, and (4) a battery-operated insole, all (5) in a size 13 boot. (Ordinarily she wears size 7.) She carries an extra foot-warmer battery, too, stowed behind her seat. One lasts only eight hours.

She also made sure that she had her cross-country essentials:

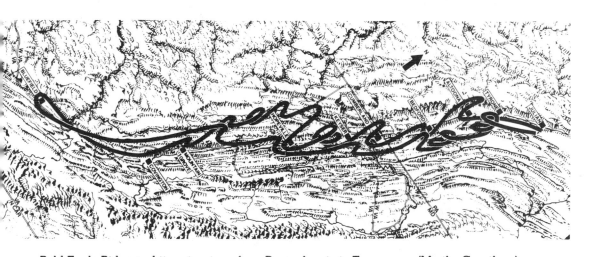

Bald Eagle Ridge and its extensions, from Pennsylvania to Tennessee. (Martha Carothers)

Barograph. To record with an inked tracing the continuous altitude of the flight—sealed, according to SSA rules, before takeoff, and to be opened only by the observer. It verifies the time that the flight took, shows the maximum height (important if an altitude record is being sought), and proves that the pilot actually was airborne during the whole time. After a successful record-breaking attempt, the barogram is sent to the Fédération Aéronautique Internationale in Paris, official recording agency. The tracing can also provide the pilot with such data as the time he spent climbing versus the time gliding, the number of thermals used, the average height flown, the total distance, and the flight efficiency —all figures to study leisurely in preparation for the *next* flight. Doris carried two barographs, just in case one didn't work.

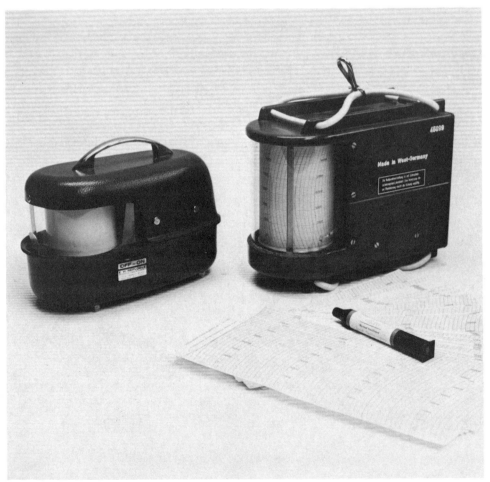

Barographs, essential to show heights and times during record flights. (Schweizer Aircraft)

Camera. The FAI also requires photographic evidence of the termination point, taken with a camera sealed and checked by the observer before and after the flight. Many a record has been disallowed because the camera failed or the pilot failed as a photographer, so record seekers often carry two cameras with them—one hand-held, the other mounted on the canopy and pointed by aiming the wing.

Parachute. SSA rules require that sailplane pilots wear parachutes in contests because of the danger of collisions when a dozen planes are circling in the same thermal. Prudence also dictates the use of parachutes in Western wave flying, where a plunge into a rotor could strip off the wings. But for ridge flying, a parachute is worthless; you're too low. Nevertheless, nearly everyone who seriously flies the ridge does use a parachute, because the seats in high-performance sailplanes are designed to accommodate them, and today's chair-type chutes are no handicap to flying. It's easier to wear one than to leave it home.

Survival kit. Some of the terrain that Doris would cross is desolate—hundreds of acres of state and national forest, uninhabited mountain property, remote swamps—and if she were to crash there, who knows when someone would find her? So just in case, she carries a survival kit, including a whistle, flashlight, metal signal mirror, plastic bottle of water, knife, compass, cigarette lighter, aspirin, bandages, and a sleeping bag in which she wraps her barographs. The whole bundle wedges behind the seat, atop a pair of normal-size hiking shoes. (With those size-13 monsters, she walks like a penguin.)

Other things also had to be attended to: She finally called Flight Service and found that winds aloft were brisk for the whole route south. She sprayed her feet with antiperspirant (to keep them warm). And she lettered a tabloid-size sign with the destination and other required information, then photographed it—another required bit of evidence for the FAI.

At six-twenty-nine, takeoff—Tom flying the towplane, Rosalie running the wing. Release: six-thirty-one at 785 feet AGL, snugged up against the ridge. For these long-distance, mostly ridge-lift flights when daylight is at a premium, takeoff should be as early as possible—just enough light to see to land again if need be. But Doris was eighteen minutes behind schedule, a delay that at the end of the day could be costly. Nevertheless, she felt great. "I was rested, eager, raring to go."

Then, immediately, trouble. The gear wouldn't rise. She tugged and pushed and hit the handle, but it wouldn't budge. A lowered gear would slow

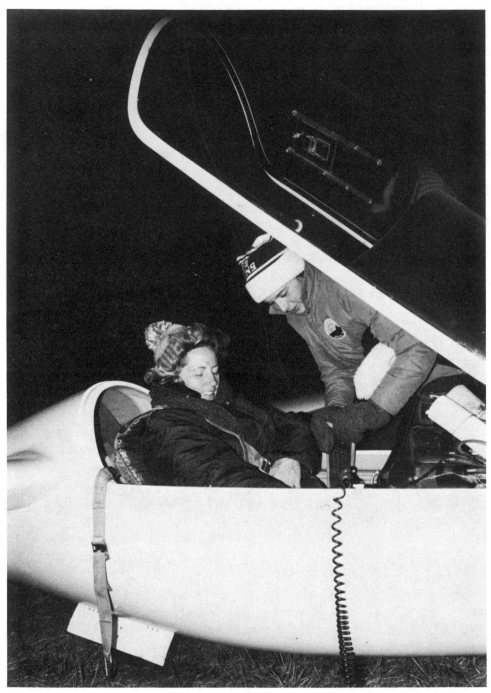

Rosalie Grove tucks her mother into the cockpit as the Bald Eagle Ridge begins to silhouette in the dawn.

her down, making the run impossible. And she was already late; landing, fixing the gear, and taking off again simply would use up too much time. "I was wasting a great deal of energy, too, yanking on that thing," she said later. "I was worried; would I have the energy and stamina for the flight?" She pulled once more, twisting, and suddenly whatever was holding it let loose; the wheel snapped into place with a reassuring thump. Doris shoved the nose down and headed southwest.

Now she settled down to flying, ridding her mind of the turmoil of getting ready, concentrating on the atmosphere around her. If the goal had been nearer she would have taken a little time to test the air, to work the ridge a bit to determine just what the wind was doing, but she had 1,000 kilometers to go, so she pushed her stick forward as far as possible without losing altitude, and skimmed the ridge top at 100 mph, wing tips flapping through the turbulence in graceful sweeps.

Meanwhile, six miles down the ridge from the airport, another long-distance pro was readying his AS-W 20 on his own mountaintop landing strip. He, too, had been watching the weather reports: Karl Striedieck, winner of four national championships, and a 1978 and 1981 member of the United States international team. He also holds the world's long-distance O&R record (1,016 miles), and he hates to let a good ridge day pass unflown. When Doris zoomed by, she was not surprised to see Striedieck's plane out on the runway, ready; she *was* surprised that he wasn't already in the air. "Karl is by far the best pilot in the U.S. today," says Doris, sharing an opinion widely held. For his part, Striedieck has kind things to say about Grove too: "She's one of the best ridge pilots there are. I'd put her among the top ten in the whole world, male or female."

Striedieck has done as much as anyone to establish Bald Eagle Ridge and its southern extensions as the best long-distance soaring range in the world. Although the ridge was flown during the twenties and thirties by such famous soaring pilots as Richard du Pont, nobody really explored its potential until Striedieck cleared his mountaintop field in 1966, then with a secondhand, moderate-performance Ka-8, amazed the soaring world by flying a world-record 476-mile O&R—at the wrong time of the year in the wrong part of the country in the wrong ship. Since then he's lost the title and regained it six times. Now he's planning one of the grandest assaults of all: a flight from central Pennsylvania all the way to Florida.

Little of this crossed Doris's mind, of course, for she was busy; just beyond Striedieck's place, the sky, which had been growing lighter, suddenly turned olive. Snow began to stream over her canopy. A little snow ordinarily is of no concern, but in this case it meant the possibility of problems at Altoona, where the ridge gaps for four miles. Because of the prevailing wind, getting across the gap from the northeast usually isn't difficult. (Coming back is.) But you do have to see, and in a heavy snow shower, you can't. That's the one thing about which Striedieck cautions visiting fliers: "I tell them to stay the hell away from snow. It could get so dense that you couldn't see the ridge, and then what are you going to do? You're going to crash, that's what."

Doris edged in closer to the ridge to make sure a sudden increase in snow wouldn't cut off her view, and in claustrophobic murkiness she tunneled on. Down below Tyrone, the ridge begins to spread out and flatten, and soon it would disappear altogether, she knew. Her altitude now was only about 200 feet above the 2,500-foot-high ridge, and from past experience she knew she needed at least a 500-foot excess. She would have to wait until the snow shower passed, then simply weave back and forth along the ridge until she located a thermal— difficult (but not impossible) to find at 7:00 A.M.

And then suddenly, as the snow shower ceased, and just at the end of the ridge, she found herself rising higher and higher in that silky smoothness that can mean only one thing: wave. With her nose pointing down, and with her speed nearing 105 mph, she sailed across the four-mile gap smoothly, silently, swiftly, and rising all the time. The wave was probably a secondary, the second harmonic of a standing wave perhaps a dozen miles northwest. As she neared the ridge on the gap's far side, she touched 5,000 feet AGL. But the wave was heading off in the wrong direction, so she coasted down to ridge lift again.

Now she was at the *second* critical gap: Bedford, Pennsylvania. And there she stopped short. "The gap is about eleven miles across," she says, "so if you don't start across at 3,500 MSL, you have to make sure you find either a thermal or wave—and I couldn't find either. I'd poke my nose out in the open, lose a couple of hundred feet, then scurry back to the ridge again." There *was* an alternative. Another, lower ridge heads south, then sweeps up northward again to meet the ridge across the gap. But it was a gamble: Lift is usually erratic, and taking that route would add an extra twenty minutes.

Making one of those decisions that would either work or kill the trip, Doris decided to try to go across. "You can fiddle around only so long," she says, "and then you have to make up your mind. I figured that if I could leave the ridge and penetrate west and upwind, keeping up as close to those low clouds as I could, I might be able to porpoise along, sort of just hang in there long enough for the wind to blow me over to the far ridge. So at one point I said out loud, 'Okay— now! Make it or land.' "

A sailplane pilot going after records or trying to win a contest must have within him the proper mixture of aggressiveness and caution. He must take chances. Yet he's got to have sense, to know when to hold back, when to be conservative. Of the two qualities, boldness is by far the scarcer. Doris has it, and so does Karl. Says he: "I guess I'm just highly competitive. There's a drive there to finish, to take chances, to go where others might hesitate. Glider pilots are sometimes afraid to go above clouds, for instance; they find it an alien world. But it doesn't bother me; if I have options and if I know there's some distance between the mountains and the cloud bottoms, I don't mind flying above a solid overcast. If I'd get stuck I'd simply pull out the spoilers, let go of the stick and let the plane muddle down through in what's called a benign spiral."

Doris's explanation is less complicated: "I just want to do it *so bad.* . . ."

And now she was aiming for the ridge on the other side of Bedford. She'd penetrate a bit, then ride zero sink for a while just at the edge of stall, then lose altitude, then move forward—and then finally she squeezed across to grab the ridge lift at the next mountain's base, rose up the side, and plunged forward again.

"I was feeling pretty good then," she says, "and even though I was being bounced around, I was able to maintain a speed of between 105 and 125 mph." The speed to fly in ridge lift is fairly easy to determine: as fast as you can go without losing altitude and without becoming too battered. One thing that Sunday-afternoon soarers don't realize is the massive punishment the human body may take on some long runs. Even though the pilot is well padded (*one* advantage of midwinter flying) and even though, snug as a finger in a thimble, the pilot hasn't room to bounce around much, the bumps as the plane sails through turbulence at 145 mph can be severe, and even in summer some pilots wear padded hats to soften slams against the canopy. Sometimes a rhythm is established: Perhaps every fifteen seconds or so the plane suddenly crashes through an invisible barrier, so the pilot speeds for ten seconds, then pulls the nose up, tenses, smacks through, then lowers the nose again. The plane can take this, but sometimes the pilot cannot. Such a workout can exhaust even the best athlete, and in times like those the sailplane pilot comes to realize that the joy of soaring isn't always in the act itself, but in having done it.

But Doris wasn't feeling fatigue yet. She couldn't even consider it, for she was preoccupied with passing over an area made for neither amateurs nor cowards. This was a section of ridge stretching from Cumberland, Maryland, past Keyser, West Virginia, a twenty-mile piece called the Knobblies, where the ridge shrinks to a dotted line of hills too low and rounded to generate strong lift—and there are few places to land if the lift disappears entirely. The few farms are small, usually on steep, gullied hills, and all bordered by tall trees, cliffs, or power lines. Here a pilot should get high enough to spot potential landing places, high enough to get to them.

And that points out one of the reasons Doris is so good: She *knows* that, knows that in this particular section one can't expect constant lift, even in ideal winds. She knows it for three reasons: First, she's soared this part of the ridge at least a dozen times. Second, she's flown it as a passenger in a power plane— watching the contours, figuring out what the wind might do if coming from various directions, taking notes, memorizing. "There are countless things I wouldn't have known otherwise," she says. "For instance, in one spot the main ridge simply stops. Another ridge continues southeast of it, but you have to switch over about two miles from the end of the main ridge, and you can see that only from altitude, not from down there on the ridge."

And third, as an instructor, she flies the ridge near her own field almost every day, and along Bald Eagle the prevailing wind generates *some* lift about a third of the flyable days. Doris has flown it so much that she subconsciously knows that when wind is blowing from *that* angle at about *this* speed over those kinds of conifers, with that kind of rock formation, there should be lift right over *there*. And even when she's in new territory on the ridge, at least it's a part of *her* ridge, and the winds behave.

The Knobblies were providing Doris with increasingly poor lift, and she was trying to decide what to do: Should she continue to look for ridge lift, or try for thermals? Most experts feel that it is better to detour even a considerable distance off the intended course if that means finding strong thermals, rather than to piddle along at minimum sink, struggling to stay aloft on weak ones. But on this day, any thermals were hidden, and Doris was worried that if she moved out to where they might be, she'd find nothing.

It was a problem that required concentration, so she flew absorbed in her task, alone, isolated, the only person in the universe. "Then suddenly, out of the corner of my eye I saw a movement," she says, "and there was Karl, zooming right out from under me and waving. Really scared me."

Striedieck went bouncing off across the Knobblies, using the minuscule ridge lift and occasionally finding a thermal—and Doris would have done the same thing except that suddenly she found herself in wave again, lifted ever so gently upward over Striedieck, 6,000 feet up, up to within 500 feet of the top of the wave cloud. But the lift was not quite strong enough to lift her *over* it, and the cloud was blocking her path. So again she had to come to a decision. Should she lose altitude and go under the cloud, probably abandoning the wave? Or should she stab right into it, risking disorientation on the one hand and possible buffeting from the rotor on the other? "I said to myself, you just have to decide, and now! I really didn't want to lose all that altitude, especially over this weak area, so I decided to plunge right in."

She was lucky. The cloud she jumped into was not a wave cloud after all (the wave cloud was probably off to the side, or perhaps it just happened to dissipate as she got up there). It was just the first of a series of broken cumulus, and so she went into one, out the other side, into another, out its other side, through perhaps a dozen. When she left the last one, she caught a thermal to circle in, floating and relaxing, then sailed down to catch the ridge again. And then, suddenly, just outside Hopewell, West Virginia, she picked up wave again—"just stumbled into it"—and soared to 13,000 feet. "At that height you have to watch closely so you don't get lost," she says. "The land seems to flatten out, and the ridge grows small, merging with the others running along together." But the altitude was good for both her spirits and her temperature. All the clothing was fine in a frigid Pennsylvania morning, but now, with midday Virginia sunshine streaming through her canopy, she welcomed the high-altitude chill.

Up here, for just a few minutes, she acted like an amateur. She got so interested in the scenery that she let her speed drop to a leisurely 70 mph when she should have been speeding. She noticed it, frowned and slammed the stick forward, quickly redlining it at 144 mph.

For 65 miles she alternated between wave and ridge lift, and thermaling every so often (at about 55 mph) for variety. When she passed over Mountain Grove, Virginia, she had a thought: Had this been early in 1968 she could turn around and go home, for she would have just bettered the world O&R record—man or woman.

Now, down on the ridge again, Doris was in territory that she had never before soared, so she kept glancing back, trying to remember what the terrain looked like so she would recognize it on the way home. She also had a chart of the region, prepared by expert sailplane pilot George Vakkur, who had flown the ridge three years before. He had marked the chart in red to show those ridges on which he had discovered usable lift. On this lap, Doris verified that the ridge was high and unbroken—perfect for speed. "So I put the nose down even further, tightened my shoulder straps, slid down into my seat to keep my head from hitting the canopy, and *went* at redline for about seventy miles."

Until *wham!* she hit a bump. Her water bottle and charts flew up, slammed against the canopy, then flopped down across her thighs just as the plane pitched forward. They ended up lodged down by the rudder pedals. She didn't care about the maps; she could get along okay without them. But the water bottle, that was different. First, it was a hazard; it could work around so that a pedal could jam. And second, she would be getting thirsty soon. On another trip the water bottle had dropped behind the seat, and she had become so obsessed with the fact that she couldn't drink, she says, that she almost aborted the flight.

So now she must get that bottle. She tried to reach it. Not even close. She tried to kick it up. Not enough room. She tried to pull up her pants leg, hoping that the bottle would ride too. The cuff was too tight. The only answer: Lift up the ship's nose and let gravity do the work. So she pulled up, up, up, and the bottle came tumbling down—just as the plane stalled. From 144 mph to a stall.

Down went the nose again as she raced forward, for there in front of her was a jog in the ridge called Jesse's Knob, and beyond it, a 290-foot tower that marked the ridge opposite Bluefield—and just beyond that, the Fincastle Country Club. Goal.

She wheeled around the club and took two photos of its roof, then circled in the other direction, snapping two more with the other camera. She's a lousy photographer, she says, and must hedge her bets. Others would simply say she's smart.

She could have, if she decided to, kept right on going in an attempt to establish the women's straight-out record for distance. Adela Dankowska of Poland had flown a record 520 miles in 1977 that still held, and to beat that, Doris would have had to keep going for only another 211 miles. But the ridge disappears farther to the south, and a sailplane pilot would have to rely exclusively on thermals. This was not a good thermal day. Besides, a landing in Tennessee would require an awfully long retrieve.

So she stood the plane on its wing, swung around northeast again, and aided by a magnificent tail wind, sped back toward Covington.

And then, a little north of Mountain Grove, problems. Bolar Mountain sits about two miles out in front of the ridge, blocking it. Doris, coming in relatively low, was faced with a choice between trying to get out to that mountain to pass around the upwind side and trying to find enough lift on the ridge, even though it was in the mountain's wind shadow.

She opted to stay on the ridge, and immediately knew she was in trouble. "The wind wasn't coming from anywhere in particular," she says, "just sort of swirling and eddying, and swirling me around, too, squeezing me down, then throwing me up, then beating me down, just beating me. I looked out my right-hand window and saw stumps of trees and rock slides only a hundred, maybe only fifty feet away. That was OK. But then I looked out my *left* side and saw the same thing, and that was not. I was on an indentation running along the side of the hill. I didn't know what the wind was doing, I was quickly running out of even minimal lift, and I didn't have much speed. I was really depressed. I picked out a field down on the valley floor and planned my landing pattern, because I was sure that I would have to land. I felt awful."

Suddenly the nibble of an updraft. Then another, and she ascended. But so did the ridge at this point, and she still didn't know if she would have enough height to clear it. But somehow she managed to slalom through the peaks and crags, and finally caught just enough updraft to lift her clear.

A dangerous time, but part of the game. Grenville Seibels, competition sailplane pilot from South Carolina, once said that in cross-country soaring "nearly every inflight decision entails some degree of deliberate, controlled risk-taking. Bad decision at altitude can usually be corrected; but down low, there is no room for error."

Now, at midafternoon, Doris was beginning to feel the strain. Her body was cramped from sitting in one position for almost a full working day. Her shoulder muscles were sore from fighting the bounces. And her flying skill had deteriorated; every so often she noticed PIOs—pilot-induced oscillation—as the plane would continue to rock or nod after a bump. Like a beginner on tow, she was overcompensating, and if she had held her right hand out before her, she would have seen it quake. Driving forward at this speed, she thought, was like racing down an interstate of potholes.

Her concentration was going too. Her mind began to wander, and then to center on herself—a common problem among long-distance sailplane pilots. They get tired, fatigue causes their judgment to be a little off, their basic flying skill becomes a shade sloppy, and they start to worry: "What's happening to me? Am I *that* out of shape? Maybe I'm losing my grip. . . ." At one point, when Doris found that she was thinking about something other than her environment, she told herself aloud to shape up: "*Concentrate*. This is serious! You've come too far to blow it now."

Hour after hour after hour of intense concentration, of constant decision making, of total attunement to a job, can warp judgment. At the Bedford gap Doris tried to read the clouds, looking for thermals. "Strange," she thought. "They're parallel to the ridge, not perpendicular like cloud streets are supposed to be." She more or less blundered into a thermal that took her high enough to barely make it across. It was only as she neared the other side that she realized why the clouds were parallel to the ridge. "Of *course* they were," she said later. "They were part of a wave, not a cloud street. I was just too tired to read them."

Doris did avoid one problem that plagues most pilots: stretched bladder. Men have a relatively easy time of it. The solution takes forethought, dexterity and patience, but a man can fill a plastic bag, then simply drop it out the window. (There are also devices that can be strapped on beforehand, but most sailplane pilots feel they're more trouble than they're worth.)

But women have a considerably more difficult time. At least one company makes a system for women pilots, but according to Doris, the device doesn't work. "A friend tried it while riding in a car," she says, "and she got herself soaking wet." That's one thing you don't want to do in a plane flying through subzero weather. What most cross-country women do is forgo drinking the night before a flight. And although they carry water in the plane, they only sip it, augmenting it with apples, celery, and other watery food. Doris has another trick, too: She averts her head when passing large bodies of water. "When I come to that big lake below Keyser," she says, "I just can't look, because if I do, water is all I can think about for the next fifteen minutes."

One serious problem with cutting down on water intake, however, is the possibility of dehydration, especially in warm weather. It can lead to fatigue, weakness, nausea, and confusion—all, of course, potentially disastrous.

The flight is over, the world record secured, and Doris Grove, exhausted, stands clutching the battery of her electrically warmed boots. (Dick Brown, State College, PA)

Now, with a surplus of time (she was an hour ahead of schedule), one more gap to go: Altoona, tough on the way back north. Without thermals, you need about 2,500 feet above the valley floor to comfortably coast the four miles and still grab the ridge. And at the wind-down of the day, you usually don't have that much height. But Doris was in for a surprise: no problem at all. A high start and a jump to the middle, a thermal that she didn't even need ("just for safety, for comfort"), and another hop to the ridge.

It was then, for the first time, that she knew she was going to make it. From Altoona on, it was her own back yard. As she passed Striedieck's place—his plane was sitting on the runway again, as though it hadn't moved that day—she was singing, loudly and not very well, a song made up on the spot: "Comin' home again—a thousand kilos behind me, and comin' home again. . . ."

She spent 9.5 hours in the air averaging 57.2 mph on the way out, 73 mph coming home, varying her AGL altitude from perhaps 75 feet to 12,000. Many others will better the distance—Doris herself, in fact—but as she was to say much later, "I was the first. No other woman will ever again be the *first* to do 1,000 kilometers."

Epilogue

But wait—outside my study window the sky has cleared. Where this morning it was sagging with walrus-colored clouds, now it's broken, and the early-afternoon sun bleaches mounds of cotton to the color of a pear tree's inner bark. And over there, toward the edge of the Allegheny Plateau, the wind blows steady from the northwest, and it looks like—it *is*—a wave beginning to build. This is no time to be working. . . .

Appendix A

Great Feats and All-Time Records

1868	La Bris & Coachman	Lifted by kite.
1884	John J. Montgomery	Glided 600 feet in Otay, California.
1891	Otto Lilienthal	Glided 1,300 feet; usually cited as the practical beginning of gliding.
1896	A. M. Herring	Glided 927 feet in a 48-second flight.
1902	Wright Brothers	One flight of 1,021 feet, others in 36-mph winds.
1905	John J. Montgomery	Dropped in a biplane-glider from a balloon at 4,000 feet; Santa Clara, California.
1911	Orville Wright	Soloed across dunes at Kitty Hawk for 9 minutes, 45 seconds.
1912	Hans Gutermuth	Flew 2,740 feet on the Wasserkuppe.
1920	Wolfgang Klemperer	Flew 1.1 miles on the Wasserkuppe.
1921	Wolfram Hirth	At second international meet in Germany, established new time record of 22 minutes.
1921	Wolfgang Klemperer	At same meet rose to 6,000 feet.
1921	Wolfgang Klemperer	First predetermined destination: 3 miles. Germany.
1922	Eddie Allen	First American participant in a world meet.
1924	Ferdinand Schulz	Rositten, Germany, eight-hour flight.
1926	Max Kegal	Sucked up into thunderhead.
1927	Ferdinand Schulz	Rositten, Germany, 283,05 miles in 14 hours, 7 minutes, in closed circuit.
1928	Peter Hesselbach	At Cape Cod, kept aloft for more than 4 hours.
1929	Ralph Barnby	Received first C Soaring Certificate issued in the United States.

1929	Robert Kronfeld	At Wasserkuppe, flew in thunderstorm for 85.5 miles at top altitude of 7,525 feet. Received first Silver award. (Hitler took it away from him and gave it to an Aryan.)
1930	Frank Hawks	Tow from San Diego to New York City in a Franklin utility prototype, *Eaglet*.
1930	Ralph Barnaby	Dropped from Navy dirigible U.S.S. *Los Angeles* at Lakehurst, New Jersey.
1931	J. K. O'Meara	Released at 3,800 feet to become the first to soar above the heart of Manhattan, circling Chrysler Building and rising to 5,000 feet.
1931	Robert Kronfeld	After 6,000-foot-high tow, glided across English Channel.
1933	Kurt Schmidt	Duration record: 36 hours, 35 minutes along dunes near Koenigsberg, East Prussia.
1933	Robert Kronfeld	Carried 200 pounds of mail from Vienna to Semmering (87 miles) in 1 hour, 40 minutes.
1933	J. K. O'Meara	Looped glider 46 times.
1934	Heini Dittmar	Near Rio de Janeiro, soared through three layers of cumulus clouds to more than 14,000 feet.
1934	Hanna Reitsch	Same occasion, set women's altitude record of 7,040 feet.
1935	Lewin Barringer	155-mile ridge flight from Ellenville, New York, to Piketown, Pennsylvania.
1937	Peter Riedel	Soared for seven hours above New York City.
1939	O. Klepikova	Russian woman established world distance record of 465 miles.
1939	Ted Bellak	Soared 56 miles across Lake Michigan to Frankfort, Michigan.
1946	John Robinson	Won three U.S. National contests in a row—1940, 1941, 1946.
1956	Paul MacCready	First American world champion.
1976	Charles Shaw	Flew 429 straight-line miles in a 1-26.

Appendix B

Soaring Records (As of 1981)

Most of the material in this Appendix, in Appendix C (Soaring Sites and Clubs), and in Appendix F (Foreign Sailplane Associations) was taken from the Soaring Society of America's annual *Membership Handbook*, and is used here by permission of the society.

OPEN SINGLE-PLACE		OPEN MULTIPLACE	
World Record	U.S. National Record	World Record	U.S. National Record
DISTANCE			
907.7 mi (1460.8 km) West Germany H. W. Grosse AS-W 12 4-25-72	716.952 mi (1153.821 km) Wallace Scott Benjamin Greene AS-W 12 7-26-70 Odessa, Texas	602.97 mi (970.4 km) Australia Ingo Renner Caproni 1-28-75	500.64 mi (805.7 km) Joseph C. Lincoln 2-32 4-30-67 Prescott, Arizona
GOAL			
779.36 mi (1254.26 km) New Zealand David Speight S. H. Georgeson Bruce L. Drake Nimbus 2 1-14-78	605.23 mi (974.04 km) Wallace Scott AS-W 12 8-22-69 Odessa, Texas	537.33 mi (864.86) West Germany I. Gorokova Blanik 6-3-67	408.9 mi (657.9) Kenneth Arterburn Lark 8-13-78 Woodsboro, Texas
OUT AND RETURN			
1015.81 (1634.7 km) U.S.A. Karl H. Striedieck AS-W 17 5-9-77	Same Lock Haven, Pennsylvania	621.54 mi (1000.05 km) Tom Knauff (pilot) Robert Gannon (passenger) GROB Astir 9-28-81 Ridge Soaring, Pennsylvania (pending)	Same

World Record	U.S. National Record	World Record	U.S. National Record
GAIN OF HEIGHT			
42,303 ft (12,894 m)	Same Lancaster, California	38,320 (11,680 m)	34,426 (10,493)
U.S.A. Paul F. Bikle 1-23E 2-25-61		Poland S. Josefczak Bocian 11-5-66	Laurence Edgar Pratt-Read 3-19-52 Bishop, California
ABSOLUTE ALTITUDE			
46,267 (14,102 m)	Same Lancaster, California	44,255 (13,489)	Same Bishop, California
U.S.A. Paul F. Bikle 1-23E 2-25-61		U.S.A. Laurence Edgar Pratt-Read 3-19-52	
SPEED OVER 100-KM—TRIANGULAR COURSE			
108.7 mph (175 kmph) South Africa Klass Goudriaan	102.742 mph (165.348 kmph) Ken Briegleb Kestrel 7-18-74 El Mirage, California	91.45 mph (147.190 kmph) South Africa Edward Mouat-Biggs Janus 11-21-77	72.932 mph (117.372 kmph) Joseph C. Lincoln 2-32A 5-24-71 Blanca, Colorado
SPEED OVER 300-KM—TRIANGULAR COURSE			
98.11 mph (157.8 kmph) Hans-Werner Grosse AS-W 17 12-24-80 Alice Springs, Australia	92.5 mph (148.83 kmph) James Nance LS-3 6-22-80 Taos, New Mexico	87.23 mph (140.48 kmph) Edwin Muller Otto Schaffner Janus 11-30-79 Certified to F.R. Germany	80.0 mph (128.72 kmph) David Allen Janus 4-17-81 Black Forest, Colorado

World Record	U.S. National Record	World Record	U.S. National Record
SPEED OVER 500-KM—TRIANGULAR COURSE			
88.88 mph (143.04 kmph)	77.65 mph (124.93 kmph)	87.03 mph (140.068 kmph)	59.6 mph David Allen (Pilot) Anson Allen (Passenger)
South Africa Edward Pearson Nimbus 2 11-27-76 74.55 mph (119.95 kmph) James Nance LS-3 5-18-81 Estrella, Arizona	Carl Herold AS-W 12 7-18-79 Air Sailing, NV	South Africa Edward Mouat-Biggs Janus 11-17-77	Janus 8-8-78 Black Forest, Colorado
SPEED OVER 750-KM—TRIANGULAR COURSE			
87.69 mph (141.13 kmph) South Africa George Eckle 1-7-78	65.8 mph Wally Scott AS-W 20 7-11-80 Odessa, Texas	81.87 mph (131.85 kmph) H. W. Grosse/ H. H. Kohlmeier SB-10 1-14-80 Australia Certified to R.F.A. F.R. Germany	None established
485 mi (780.37 km) 55.8 mph (89.78 kmph) Wally Scott AS-W 20 7-11-81 Odessa, Texas			
SPEED OVER 1000-KM—TRIANGULAR COURSE			
90.32 mph (145.32 kmph) West Germany Hans-Werner Grosse 1-3-79	57 mph (91.71 kmph) Thomas Knauff Nimbus 2 4-2-81 Ridge Soaring, Pennsylvania	129.54 kmph (80.44 mph) H. W. Grosse/ H. H. Kohlmeier SB-10 12-12-79 Australia Certified to F.R. Germany	None established

World Record	U.S. National Record	World Record	U.S. National Record

SPEED OVER 1250-KM (789.89-MILE)—TRIANGULAR COURSE

82.74 mph
(133.13 kmph)
Hans-Werner Grosse
AS-W 17
Alice Springs, Australia
12-12-80
Certified to R.F.A.
  F.R. Germany
(pending)

DISTANCE AROUND A TRIANGULAR COURSE

811 miles	621.36 miles	690.93 miles	None established
(1,306 km)	(1000.58 km)	(1112.62 km)	
West Germany	Thomas Knauff	H. W. Grosse/	
Hans-Werner Grosse	Nimbus 2	H. H. Kohlmeier	
AS-W 17	4-2-81	SB-10	
1-4-81	Ridge Soaring,	12-28-79	
Alice Springs,	Pennsylvania	Australia	
Australia		Certified to R.F.A.,	
(pending)		F.R. Germany	

SPEED OVER AN OUT-AND-RETURN COURSE OF 300 KM

119.4 mph
(192.11 kmph)
Thomas Knauff
Nimbus 2
3-27-81
Ridge Soaring,
Pennsylvania
(pending)

SPEED OVER AN OUT-AND-RETURN COURSE OF 500 KM

82.55 mph
(132.82 kmph)
Thomas Knauff
Nimbus 2
11-10-80
Ridge Soaring,
Pennsylvania

51 mph
(82.06 kmph)
Ivan Jaszlics
1-34
6-21-81
Taos, New Mexico

WOMEN'S SINGLEPLACE		WOMEN'S MULTIPLACE	
World Record	U.S. National Record	World Record	U.S. National Record
DISTANCE			
589.7 mi (949.7 km) Australia Karla Karel 1-20-80 Certified to Great Britain	426.47 mi (686.34 km) Betsy Howell Std. Cirrus 8-27-73 Odessa, Texas	537.399 mi (864.862 km) U.S.S.R. T. Pavlova Blanik 6-3-67	170.316 mi (274.100 km) Betsy W. Proudfit Pratt-Read 7-11-52 El Mirage, California
GOAL			
454.59 mi (731.59 km) U.S.S.R. T. Zaiganova	Same	537.399 mi (864.862 km) U.S.S.R.	170.316 mi (274.100 km) Betsy W. Proudfit
		I. Gotokhova	Pratt-Read
7-29-66		Blanik	7-11-52
		6-3-73	El Mirage, California
OUT AND RETURN			
700.1 mi (1126.046 km) Doris Grove 9-28-81 AS-W 19 Ridge Soaring, Pennsylvania	Same	383.65 mi (617.29 km) Pelagia Majewska Hainy 5-14-81 Leszo, Poland	None established
GAIN OF HEIGHT			
29,918 ft (9,119 m) England A. Burns 1-13-61	27,994 ft (8,533 m) Betsy W. Proudfit Pratt-Read 4-14-55 Bishop, California	27,657 ft (8,430 m) Poland A. Dankowska Bocian 10-17-67	24,545 ft (7,481 m) B. Nutt 2-32 3-5-75 Colorado Springs, Colorado

World Record	U.S. National Record	World Record	U.S. National Record
ABSOLUTE ALTITUDE			
41,460 ft (12,637 m)	Same Black Forest, Colorado	35,463 ft (10,809 m)	Same Colorado Springs, Colorado
USA Sabrina Jackintell 2-14-79		USA B. Nutt 2-32 3-5-75	
SPEED OVER 100-KM—TRIANGULAR COURSE			
86.59 mph (139.45 kmph) Australia Susan Martin 2-2-79	76.869 mph (123.710) Leila Tweed Kestrel 40 7-18-74 El Mirage, California	78.47 mph (125.98) Poland Dankowska/Grzelak Halny 8-1-78	23.23 mph Gun-Britt Floden Blanik 5-9-76 Van Sant, Pennsylvania
SPEED OVER 300-KM—TRIANGULAR COURSE			
78.8 mph (126.79 kmph) Waikerie, Australia	60.7 mph (97.66 kmph) Sabrina Jackintell	78.87 mph (126.90 kmph)	None established
Sue Martin Ventus	Astir 7-2-78	Sue Martin Ventus	
2-2-81	Black Forest, Colorado	2-2-81	
(pending)			Waikerie, Australia (pending)
SPEED OVER 500-KM—TRIANGULAR COURSE			
82.68 mph (133.144 kmph) Australia S. Martin 1-29-79	None established	43.246 mph (69.598) U.S.S.R. T. Zaiganova Blanik 5-29-68	None established

World Record	U.S. National Record	World Record	U.S. National Record
SPEED OVER 750-KM—TRIANGULAR COURSE			
59.27 mph (95.45 kmph) Australia Elizabeth Karel 1-24-79	None established	None established	None established
SPEED OVER 1000-KM—TRIANGULAR COURSE			
None established	None established	None established	None established
DISTANCE AROUND A TRIANGULAR COURSE			
505.5 m (814.01 km) Australia Karla Karel LS-3 1-9-80 Certified to Great Britain	None established	None established	None established
SPEED OVER AN OUT-AND-RETURN COURSE OF 300 KM			
	90 mph (144.83 kmph) Doris Grove AS-W 19 9 June 81 Ridge Soaring, Pennsylvania		

Appendix C

Soaring Sites and Clubs

ALABAMA
Birmingham 35205
Birmingham Soaring Society
2101 Magnolia Avenue South

Ozark 36360
Soaring Club in Dale County
Drawer W

ALASKA
Anchorage 99502
Glacier Sky Sailing
7710 Honeysuckle Drive

Fairbanks 99071
Alaska Soaring Society
171 Hamilton Way
(Bradley Field)

ARIZONA
Phoenix 85020
Turf Soaring School
P.O. Box 1586, Black Canyon Stat.

Tempe 85282
Arizona Soaring Inc.
P.O. Box 27427

Tempe 85282
Rainco, Inc.
P.O. Box 27345

Tucson 85717
Tucson Soaring Club
P.O. Box 40155
(Ryan Field)

Yuma 85364
Yuma Soaring Association
720-9 Avenue

ARKANSAS
Arkadelphia 71923
Mid-South Soaring Inc.
1019 Pine Street

Marion 72364
Southern Soaring, Inc.
P.O. Box 330

CALIFORNIA
Adelanto 92301
El Mirage Sky Range
P.O. Box 102 El Mirage Route
(c/o Mark Thompson)

Altadena 91001
Elsinore Valley Soaring Club
1950 Midwick Drive
(Hemet-Ryan Airport)

Anaheim 92806
Phoenix Club Soaring
1566 Douglas Road
(El Mirage Field)

Brownsville 95919
Aero Pines
Brownsville Airport

Buena Park 90620
Orange County Soaring Association
P.O. Box 5475
(Perris Valley Airport)

California City 93505
Super Cub Services
Municipal Airport

Calistoga 94515
Calistoga Soaring Center
1546 Lincoln Avenue

Chico 95926
Chico Soaring Association
P.O. Box 1571
(c/o G. Casamajor)

Colton 92324
Academic Soaring Club
2100 Cahuilla
(c/o George Lessard)

Costa Mesa 92626
Avcenter Aircraft Supply
3184 Airway Avenue

Costa Mesa 92626
Cumulo-Nimbus Escadrille
2718 Sandpiper Drive

Cypress 90630
Cypress Soaring, Inc.
P.O. Box 694
(c/o Robert Morgan)

Elsinore 92330
Aerosport, Inc.
32301 Corydon Street

Fremont 94538
Sky Sailing Airport
44999 Christy Street
(c/o Bret Willat)

Hemet 92343
Sailplane Enterprises
P.O. Box 1650

Inyokern 93527
Sierra Soaring
P.O. Box 601

Irvine 92714
MK Products
16882 Armstrong Avenue

La Jolla 92093
UCSD Soaring Club
Marietta B-023

Lodi 95240
Big Valley Soaring
12145 De Vries Road
(c/o Debbie Stone)

Lake Elsinore 92330
Skylark, Southern California
32019 Corydon Road

Los Angeles 90041
Douglas Soaring Club
5224 Rockland Avenue
(c/o F. K. Nieuwenhuijs)

Livermore 94550
Northern California Soaring Association
P.O. Box 338
(Humingbird Haven)

Livermore 94550
Pacific Soaring Council
1045 Catalina Drive

Long Beach 90803
Seal Beach Naval Aero Club
39 Nieto Avenue

Long Pine 93545
Mount Whitney Soaring Inc.
P.O. Box 775

Monrovia 91016
San Gabriel Valley Soaring
131 Scenic Drive

Montague 96064
Montague Aviation
P.O. Box 128
(Rohrer Field)

Mojave 93500
Aquarian Soaring
California City Airport

Northridge 91324
Antelope Valley Soaring Club
11665 Seminole Circle
(El Marage Field)

Oakland 94614
Soaring Experience, Inc.
P.O. Box 2547 Airport Station

Pearblossom 93553
Great Western Soaring School
P.O. Box 189
(c/o Gene Jordan)

Pope Valley 94567
Pope Valley Soaring Ranch
1996 Pope Canyon Rd.

Porterville 93257
Mitchell Aircraft Corp.
1900 South Newcomb

Rosamond 93560
Aronson's Air Service
P.O. Box J
(c/o Wolfgang Wagner)

San Diego 92101
Associated Glider Clubs
of Southern California
P.O. Box 3301
(c/o Phil Dufford)

San Diego 92116
Borderland Air Sports
4627 Vista Street

San Diego 92173
Steck Aviation, Inc.
Brown Field
(c/o Jim MacDonald)

San Jose 95129
Calcondors Soaring Club
1479 Petal Way

San Rafael 94901
East Bay Soaring Club
144 Center Street

San Rafael 94903
North Bay Soaring Association
19 Farm Road
(Sonoma Skypark)

Santa Monica 90405
Graham Thomson Ltd.
3200 Airport Avenue

Sunnyvale 94087
Air Sailing
966 Astoria Drive

Tehachapi 93561
Skylark North
P.O. Box 918
(Fantasy Haven Airport)

Torrance 90505
Nagel Aircraft Sales
25320 Curtiss Way

Truckee 95734
Donner Aviation, Inc.
P.O. Box 2657

Truckee 95734
Tahoe Truckee Aviation
P.O. Box 2458

29 Palms 92277
29 Palms Soaring Club
County Airport

Vacaville 95688
Vacaville Soaring, Inc.
P.O. Box 176
(c/o David Williams)

Van Nuys 91401
Bernoulli's Soaring Association
5932 Colbath Avenue
(Fantasy Haven Airport)

Van Nuys 91406
Pan American Navigation
16934 Saticoy

Ynez 93460
Santa Ynez Valley Soaring School
P.O. Box 666

COLORADO
Arvada 80005
Denver Soaring Council
7942 Field Cr.
(Boulder Airport)

Aspen 81611
Gliders of Aspen
P.O. Box 175

Boulder 80306
The Cloud Base
P.O. Box 1651

Boulder 80306
Soaring Society of Boulder
P.O. Box 1031

Boulder 80303
Western Flight Training
Municipal Airport

Colorado Springs 80908
Johnson Aircraft
10850 Thomas Road

Colorado Springs 80908
Wave Flights, Inc.
9990 Gliderport Road

Colorado Springs 80915
High Flights Soaring Club
1525 North Lyle Drive
(Meadowlake Airport)
Durango 81301

Durango Soaring Association
31505 Highway 160

Englewood 80110
Colorado Soaring Association
1130 West Stanford Drive
(Black Forest Gliderport)

Fort Collins 80522
Waverly West Soaring Ranch
P.O. Box 1055

Grand Junction 81501
Lands End Soaring
326 Hillcrest Manor

Gunnison 81230
Rocky Warren
P.O. Box 478

USAF Academy 80840
U.S.A.F. Academy Soaring Branch
F73WIA M3579 CWIA

Wellington 80549
Rocky Mountain Soaring
P.O. Box 420
(three locations)

CONNECTICUT

Botsford 06404
Nutmeg Soaring Association
c/o Joseph Murphy,
General Delivery

Bristol 06010
Tunxis Soaring Club
c/o 40 Vantana Drive

Old Saybrook 06474
Connecticut Cu-Climbers Soaring
34 Fernwood Grove Road

Plymouth 06782
Connecticut Soaring Center
Waterbury Airport

Ridgefield 06877
Connecticut Yankee Soaring Club
34 Catoonah Street
(Canaan Airport)

DELAWARE

Salisbury, Maryland 21801
Eastern Shore Soaring Association
Laurel Airport

Wilmington 19899
Brandywine Soaring Association
P.O. Box 454

FLORIDA

Arcadia 33821
Lenox Flight School
Arcadia Airport

Brooksville 33512
Aerocraft Unlimited, Inc.
P.O. Box 999x
(c/o Ralph Robbins)

Clearwater 33515
Clearwater Soaring
1800 Drew Street

Clearwater 33520
Delta Aircraft Corp.
Clearwater Airport

Dunedin 33528
Sky Sailors Association, Inc.
1646 Pasadena Drive
(Winter Haven Airport)

Gainesville 32601
Florida Soaring Association
P.O. Box 14362,
University Station

High Springs 32643
Rudy's Gliderport
Route 1, Box 102

Jacksonville 32216
North Florida Soaring Society
7853 La Sierra Court
(Herlong Airport)

Indiantown 33456
The Soaring School
P.O. Box 566

Jacksonville 32211
Sail Planes, Inc.
1441 University Boulevard North

Miami 33197
Glades Soaring School
P.O. Box 970664
(Kendall Gliderport)

Orange Park 32073
North Florida Soaring Society
2580 Shalimar Lane

Oviedo 32765
Soaring Seminoles, Inc.
Route 1, Box 475

Owee 32761
Citrus Soaring
P.O. Box 86
(Macquire Airport)

Pensacola 32506
Coastal Soaring Association
Route 8, Box 626
(Coastal Airport)

Pompano Beach 33060
Pompano Soaring Center
1006 N.E. 11th Avenue

Quincy 32351
Aquarius Aviation, Inc.
Route 6, Box 398

Sebring 33870
Sebring Soaring Centre
Building 100, Box 499

Tallahassee 32301
Apalachee Soaring Society
2415 San Pedro Drive
(Quincy Airport)

Tampa 33612
University of Southern Florida
  Soaring Society
1907 Meridel Avenue

Tampa 33617
Winter Haven Soaring
11716 Fife Avenue
(Gilbert Field)

Vero Beach 32960
Suncoast Soaring Association
826 17th Avenue
(Hibiscus Airport)

GEORGIA
Albany 31707
Sowega Soaring Society
1511 4th Avenue

Douglas 31533
Holiday Beach Air Park
Route 2, Box 158W

Gainesville 76240
J.D.J. Flying Service
P.O. Box 756

Monroe 30655
Mid-Georgia Soaring Association
P.O. Box W

Savannah 31406
Sea Islands Soaring Society
P.O. Box 13919
(Plantation Airpark)

Williamson 30292
Peach State Gliderport
P.O. Box 52

HAWAII
Honolulu 86822
Oahu Soaring Club
1630 Liholiho Street
(Dillingham Airfield)

Waialua 96791
Skysurfing, Inc.
P.O. Box 664

Waialua 96791
Honolulu Soaring Club
P.O. Box 626
(c/o Bill Star)

IDAHO
Athol 83801
Inland Empire Soaring Council
P.O. Box 63-A

Driggs 83422
Red Baron Flying
Teton Peaks Airport

Hailey 83333
Condor Sky Sailing, Inc.
P.O. Box 1101

Sagle 83860
Inland Empire Soaring Council
P.O. Box 187

Sun Valley 83353
Sun Valley Soaring Flight
P.O. Box 248

ILLINOIS

Decatur 62525
Decatur-Moweaqua Soaring
4356 Leonore Drive
(c/o Russell Price)

Downers Grove 60515
Northern Illinois Glider Club
835 Curtiss St., Apt. 202

Hinckley 60520
Hinckley Soaring, Inc.
Hinckley Airport

Lawrenceville 62439
Wabash Valley Soaring Association
P.O. Box 287

Lockport 60441
Chicago Glider Council
c/o Route 2, Box 22

Minooka 60447
Chicago Glider Club
P.O. Box 618G
(c/o Gene Hammond)

Plainfield 60544
Windy City Soaring
Clow Airport

Urbana 61801
University of Illinois
101 Transportation Building

Olympia Fields 60461
Air Display, Inc.
1029 Wingate Road
(Haedtler Airport)

Rockford 61109
Peterson Flight School
2 Airport Circle

Rockford 61108
Northern Illinois Soaring Association
4455 East Charles #31
(c/o Gerry Sibley)

Trenton 62293
St. Lewis Soaring Association
Route 2, Box 143

INDIANA

Bloomington 47401
Hoosier Soaring Club
310 Gilbert Avenue

Kendallville 46755
Callahan Aviation, Inc.
R.R. 3
(c/o Tom Callahan)

Lafayette 47905
Lafayette Soaring Society
1145 Rochelle Drive
(Halsmer Airport)

Michigan City 46360
Aire-Dale Flying Service
R.R. 4, Box 141

Mishawaka 46544
Michiana Soaring Society
139 Manor Drive

Zionsville 46077
Central Indiana Soaring Society
Terry Airport

IOWA

Ames 50010
Silent Knights
Route 3
(c/o J. F. Smith)

Burlington 52601
Burlington Soaring Association, Inc.
16 Cascade Terrace

Davenport 52804
EAA Chapter 75 Gliding Club
c/o 1525 W. Columbia Avenue

Des Moines 50309
Central Iowa Soaring Society, Inc.
935 Insurance Exchange

Durant 52747
EAA Chapter 75 Glider Club
702 8th Street

Nevada 50201
Aeronautique
1207 H Avenue

KANSAS

Hutchison 67501
Silent Soarers, Inc.
13 Whitmore Road

Topeka 66618
Mesa Verde Airport
5225 NW 62nd Street

Wichita 76208
Kansas Soaring Association
115 North Crestway
(Sunflower Aerodrome)

Wichita 67228
Air Capital Soaring Enterprise
135 East 45th Street North
(c/o Fay Edwards)

KENTUCKY

Irvine 40336
Central Kentucky Soaring
Route 4, Box 178

Paducah 42101
Farrington Aircraft Corp.
Farrington Airpark

Louisville 40222
Louisville Soaring Club
2825 Murry Hill Pike

LOUISIANA

Alexandria 71301
Magnolia Airways, Inc.
4112 Leon Drive

Covington 70433
Louisiana Soaring
P.O. Box 1173

Monroe 71201
Aero-Nutz
P.O. Box 4151

Pinesville 73160
Central Louisiana Soaring Society
605 Hilliday Circle

Shreveport 71105
Shreveport Soaring Club
2055 Bermuda

MAINE

Concord 01742
Cambridge Aero Inst.
365 Old Marlboro Road

Lynn 01903
Northeastern Light Aircraft
Box 252

Turner 04282
Turner Soaring, Inc.
c/o Greg Randall, Route 4

MARYLAND

Cumberland 21502
Cumberland Soaring Club
P.O. Box 866
(c/o J. F. Wagner)

Frederick 21701
Mid-Atlantic Soaring Association
4823 Teen Barnes Road
(c/o Hope Howard)

Patuxent River 20670
Patuxent Navy Flying Club
P.O. Box 5, NAS

Stevensville 21666
Chesapeake Soaring
Bay Bridge Airport

MASSACHUSETTS

Berkshire 01224
Berkshire Soaring Society
P.O. Box 103 Gulf Road
(Pittsfield Municipal Airport)

North Hatfield 01066
Pilgrim Soaring Center
P.O. Box 4

New Braintree 01531
New England Soaring Association
Hiller Airport

Plymouth 02360
Gliding Club of Boston
Plymouth Airport

Reading 01867
M.I.T. Soaring Association
12 Audubon Road
(Mansfield Airport)

Sterling 01565
Greater Boston Soaring Club
Sterling Airport

Wellesley 02181
Mount Washington Soaring
46 Leewood Road

MICHIGAN
Frankfort 49635
Frankfort Aviation
Frankfort Airport

Frankfort 49635
Northwest Soaring Club
P.O. Box 88

Ionia 48846
Benz Aviation
Ionia County Airport

Pontiac 48057
Drake Aviation Co.
4251 Giddings Road

Saginaw 48601
Saginaw Valley Soaring
c/o 314 Linton Street

Van Dyke 48003
Almont School of Aviation
4296 Van Dyke

MINNESOTA
Mankato 55060
Mankato Soaring
Mankato Airport

Marshall 49068
Eagle's Nest Soaring
P.O. Box 310

Minneapolis 55409
Minn. Assn. of Soaring Clubs
3901 Harriet Avenue South

Minneapolis 55417
Red Wing Soaring Association
5129 42nd Avenue South
(c/o Harris Hollen)

Minneapolis 55407
White Bear Gliding
#310 2809 Park Avenue

Owatonna 55060
Soar, Inc.
Owatonna Airport

Stanton 55081
Minnesota Soaring Club
Carleton Airport

St. Paul 55107
The Pilot Shop
St. Paul Downtown Airport

Thief River Falls 56701
Northern Soaring, Inc.
118 North Kendall

MISSISSIPPI
Bay St. Lewis 39520
Bay Aviation, Inc.
Route 3, Box 987

Mendenhall 39114
Mississippi Soaring Association
c/o 108 Ellis Street

Mississippi State University 39762
State College Glider Club
Box 4642

MISSOURI
Jefferson City 65101
Skylark, Inc.
P.O. Box 515

Kansas City 64151
Midwestern Soaring Association
6020 North Gower
(c/o James Brewster)

Springfield 65802
Springfield Hawks Soaring Association
1717 West Nichols
(c/o Gary Stepp)

St. Charles 63301
St. Charles Flying Service
St. Charles Airport

St. Louis 93520
Bay Aviation
Stennis International Air Bay

Warrensburg 64093
Central Missouri State University
   Soaring Club
Sky Haven Airport

MONTANA

Belgrade 59714
Bridger Mountain Soaring
P.O. Box 808
(Gallatin Field)

Kalispell 59901
Holman Aviation
P.O. Box 218

Red Lodge 59068
Red Lodge Airways
P.O. Box 447

NEBRASKA

Lincoln 68501
Frelin Soaring Association
P.O. Box 83208

McCook 69001
McCook Soaring Association
c/o Box 491

Scottsbluff 69361
Panhandle Soarers
3610 Avenue D

Sioux City 68776
Sioux Air, Inc.
P.O. Box 425

NEVADA

Carson City 89701
Carson Valley Flight Service
701 Highland

Boulder City 89005
Desert Soaring of Boulder
P.O. Box 637

Las Vegas 89119
Terra Training
5616 South Haven
(Jean Airport)

Minden 89423
Casino Air, Inc.
P.O. Box 629

Reno 89506
Sierra-Nevada Soaring
P.O. Box 60036

Reno 89510
Silver State Soaring
Star Route 1

NEW HAMPSHIRE

Franconia 03580
Franconia Aviation
c/o Franconia Inn

New London 03257
Kearsarge Soaring Association
Shaker Road
(c/o Harold Smith)

North Conway 03860
Mt. Washington Soaring Association
White Mountain Airport

NEW JERSEY

Blairstown 07060
Icarus Soaring Club
Blairstown Airport

Milford 08848
Cumulus Ridge Farm
Route 2, Box 169

Nutley 07110
Tocks Island Soaring
361 Walnut Street

Pittstown 08867
Airborne Arts
RD 2, Box 22A

Princeton 08544
Soaring Society of Princeton University
c/o Barry Nixon,
Flight Research Laboratory

Robbinsville 08691
TRA Soaring Center
108 Sharon Road

South Bound Brook 08880
Aero Club Albatross
Box 174
(c/o Diana DeLange)

Titusville 08560
Central Jersey Soaring Club
1 Barbara Lane

Vineland 08360
South Jersey Soaring Club
Box 489

NEW MEXICO

Albuquerque 87192
Albuquerque Soaring Club
P.O. Box 11254

Hobbs 88240
Hobbs Soaring Society
P.O. Box 274

Los Lunas 87032
Valley High Soaring
212 Los Familias

Wayne 07470
Valley Soaring
42 Lenape

NEW YORK

Bronx 10457
Sailflights, Inc.
4422 Third Avenue

Cooperstown 13326
Iroquois Soaring Association
P.O. Box 292

Dansville 14437
Dansville Soaring Club
Dansville Municipal Airport

Endicott 13760
Perrucci Aviation
310 East Main Street

Endicott 13760
Tri Cities Soaring Society
Tri-Cities Airport

Elmira 14902
Schweizer Soaring School
P.O. Box 147

Elmira 14903
Harris Hill Soaring Corporation
Harris Hill, RD 3

Fayetteville 13066
Thermal Ridge Soaring
115 Kittell Road

Ithaca 14850
Ithaca Soaring Club
1755 Mecklenburg Road

Jamestown 14701
Chatauqua Soaring Society
P.O. Box 2045

Mayville 14757
Aero Soaring Club
P.O. Box 107

Merrick 11566
Long Island Soaring Association
1247 Lednam Ct.
(c/o Rudolf Suehs)

New Hartford 13413
Gilad Soaring Service
66 Root Street

New York 10005
American International Insurance
70 Pine Street

Rochester 14615
Glider Pilot's Ground School
69 Rhea Crescent

Schenectady 12304
Mohawk Soaring Club
1609 Bradley Boulevard

Shirley 11967
Sky Sailors, Inc.
222 Grand Avenue

South Cairo 12482
Catskill Valley Flying Service
P.O. Box 44

Spencerport 14616
Rochester Soaring Club
301 Whittier Road

Syracuse 13088
Soaring Club of Syracuse
512 Oswego Street

Tonawanda 14120
Niagara Soaring Club
3767 Moyer Road North
(c/o Clements Hoovler)

Wurtsboro 12790
Wurtsboro Flight Service
P.O. Box 382

NORTH CAROLINA

Albemarle 28001
Stanley Soaring School
508 N. 9th Street

Chapel Hill 27514
Meadow Lark Soaring
P.O. Box 2006

Farmville 27828
Farmville Soaring Club
P.O. Box 546

Raleigh 27650
North Carolina State University
Box 5246, NCSU
(c/o Paul West)

NORTH DAKOTA
Grand Forks 58202
University of North Dakota
P.O. Box 8216 University Station
(c/o Gunter Voltz)

OHIO
Akron 44303
Canton-Akron Soaring Club
710 Mentor Road

Brookville 45309
Brookville Airpark
R.R. 2, Route 40

Brunswick 44212
Sky Roamers Soaring Club
1676 Dorchester Drive

Columbus 43229
Central Ohio Soaring Association
5288 Butternut Ct. West
(Marian Municipal Airport)

Dayton 45409
Caesar Creek Soaring Club
P.O. Box 581

Ft. Wayne 46825
Bryan Soaring Club
915 Lemonwood Court

Elyria 44035
Fun Country Soaring
207 Stanford Avenue

Lebanon 45036
Lane's Air Service
2460 Greentree Road

Montpelier 43543
Elf Soaring Enterprises
Rural Route 3
(c/o Ed Frappier)

Niles 44446
Northern Ohio Soaring
418 Williams Street

North Canton 44730
Canton Aviation Center
5367 East Center Drive N.E.

Parma Heights 44130
Cleveland Soaring Society
6640 Pearl Road
(Chardon Airport)

OKLAHOMA
Lawton 73502
Southwest Oklahoma Soaring Association
Box 1663

Norman 73069
Silent Flight Soaring School
1133 C Biloxi

Ponca City 74601
Aerohead Aviation
P.O. Box 1808

Stillwater 74024
Oklahoma State University
Aviation Education Department

Tulsa 74101
Tulsa Skyhawks Soaring
P.O. Box 1345

OREGON
Albany 97321
Sail-Em Gliders, Inc.
2825 Willetta, Suite B

Beaverton 97005
Willamette Valley Soaring
14175 S.W. Spinnaker Drive

Eugene 97405
Emerald Valley Soaring Club
86436 Needham Road

La Grande 97850
High Flight Soaring
307 Second Street

La Grande 97850
Grande Ronde Aviation
Route 2, Box 2546

Medford 97501
Beagle Sky Ranch
P.O. Box 1661

PENNSYLVANIA

Berwick 18603
Blue Sky Sailing
RD 1, Box 22

East Stroudsburg 18301
Birchwood-Pocono Airpark
RD 3

East Stroudsburg 18301
North Star Aerosports
P.O. Box 201

Exton 19341
Cloudiners
P.O. Box 262

Erwinna 18920
Posey Aviation
Van Sant Airport

Frederick (MD) 21701
Mid-Atlantic Soaring Association
4023 Teen Barnes Rd.
(Fairfield Airport)

Julian 16844
Ridge Soaring
Ridge Soaring Gliderport

Kutztown 19530
Kutztown Aviation Service
P.O. Box 1, Route 1

Lehighton 18235
Beltzville Airport
RD 3
(c/o David Beltz)

McMurray 15317
Pittsburgh Soaring Club
111 Roscommon Place

Mercer 16137
Butler Soaring Club
Route 2, Box 2476
(c/o W. P. Jones)

Perkasie 18944
Philadelphia Glider Council
934 Route 152
(c/o Richard Wagner)

Rosemont 19010
The Soaring Dutchmen
Greenbank Road
(c/o J. W. Homeier)

Stroudsburg 18360
Kittatinny Soaring Club
908 White Street

RHODE ISLAND

Lincoln 02865
North Central Airways
North Central Airport

Peace Dale 02883
Richmond Soaring
P.O. Box 38

Providence 02965
Brown University Soaring
Student Activities Box 15

SOUTH CAROLINA

Aiken 29801
Aiken Soaring Club
106 Idlewild Drive

Chester 29706
Bermuda High Soaring
P.O. Drawer 809

Little River 29566
Carolina Sailplanes, Inc.
P.O. Box 241

SOUTH DAKOTA

Rapid City 57701
West Rivers Soarers
R.R. 4, Box 815-A

Sioux Falls 57105
Der Floeten Flieger
1112 S. Van Eps
(c/o Doc Walker)

TENNESSEE

Chattanooga 37405
Chilhower Gliderport
15 Fairhill Drive

Memphis 38112
Memphis Soaring Society
685 Cypress Drive

Nashville 37217
Eagleville Soaring School
1311 Currey Road

Rockwood 37854
Bill Dietz Aero Service
P.O. Box 4

TEXAS

Amarillo 79105
High Plains Soaring Society
P.O. Box 604
(Airsport Airport)

Austin 78758
Fault Line Flyers Glider Club
1110 Bruton Spring Road
(Georgetown Municipal Airport)

Big Spring 79721
Signal Mountain Soaring Society
c/o 2701 Cactus Drive

Brownsville 78520
Hunt Pan Am Dist.
P.O. Box 706

Caddo Mills 75005
Southwest Soaring Enterprises
P.O. Box 460

Castroville 78009
Alamo Soaring
P.O. Box 793

Dallas 75240
Dallas Gliding Association
3536 Granada

Dallas 75233
Dallas Soaring Association
c/o 3417 Canson

Ft. Worth 76133
Sky Roamers
6505 Poco Court

Ft. Davis 79734
Blue Mountain Airport
P.O. Box 595

Hearne 77859
West Wind Soaring
P.O. Box 465

Houston 77074
Houston Soaring Association
7435 Jackwood
(Kary Airport)

Houston 77096
Soaring Club of Houston
5218 Carew
(c/o Bill Fisher)

Irving 75061
North Dallas Gliders, Inc.
1929 East Grauwyler #219

McKinney 75069
Aero Country Aviation
RT 1

Midland 79701
Permian Soaring Association
c/o 3607 Sinclair Avenue

Midlothian 76065
Texas Soaring Association
P.O. Box 1069

Mission 78572
Brownsville Soaring Club
P.O. Box 873

Odessa 79762
Airmark
7000 Andrews Highway

Refugio 78377
Refugio Soaring Circle
Box 366
(Rooke Field)

Seabrook 79568
Mesilla Valley Soaring
415 Bayou View

Spicewood 78669
Windemere Soaring School
Route 2, Box 491

Tyler 75703
East Texas Soaring Club
8318 Yale Drive
(Pounds Airport)

Weatherford 76086
Western Hills Aviation
3816 Ft. Worth Highway

Woodsboro 78393
Vanair Aviation Services
P.O. Box 637

UTAH

Brigham City 84302
Brigham Soaring Association
Box 341

Cedar City 94720
Color Canyons Aviation
P.O. Box 458

Heber City 84032
Heber Valley Flying Service
RFD 1 Box 443-A

Logan 84321
Valley Airmotive Corp.
Logan-Cache Airport, Box 281

Salt Lake City 84117
Soaring Society of Utah
4589 Wallace Lane
(Heber City Airport)

Wendover 84083
Northern Nevada Aviation
Decker Field

VERMONT

Morrisville 05661
Mansfield Aviation/Stowe Soaring
Morrisville-Stowe Airport

No. Springfield 05161
Green Mountain Soaring
Springfield-Hartness Airport

No. Springfield 05161
Precision Valley Soaring
Springfield-Hartness

Post Mills 05058
Post Mills Aviation, Inc.
Box 51

Warren 05674
Sugarbush Soaring Club
c/o Sugarbush Inn

VIRGINIA

Earlysville 22936
Ridge and Valley Soaring Club
Belvedere Farms
(c/o Ron Roberts)

Richmond 23234
Soaring Unlimited
7400 White Pine Road

Salem 24153
Blue Ridge Soaring Society
P.O. Box 122

Salem 24153
New River Soaring Association
Route 4, Box 311

Warrenton 22186
Warrenton Soaring Center
P.O. Box 185

Windsor 23487
Tidewater Soaring Society
P.O. Box 86, Route 2

WASHINGTON

Colville 99114
Jey Aero
625 South Rae Street

Ellensburg 98926
Central Washington Flying
P.O. Box 345

Ellensburg 98920
Ellensburg Sport Aviation
1512 Skyline Drive

Ephrata 98823
Inland Aviation, Inc.
P.O. Box 424

Kirkland 98033
Seattle Glider Council
P.O. Box 548

Moses Lake 98837
Eastern Evergreen Enterprises
1122 Baker

Pullman 99163
Palause Hills Soaring
P.O. Box 212

Pullman 99163
Soaring Unlimited
P.O. Box 548

Richland 99352
Columbia Basin Soaring
202 Thayer

Richland 99352
Flight Incorporated
1986 Marshall

Seattle 98124
Boeing Employees Soaring
P.O. Box 3707, 4H-96

Seattle 98195
University of Washington Soaring
208 Hub Box 100 FK-10

Spokane 99220
Lesley's Sky Sailing
P.O. Box 2661

Toledo 98591
Toledo-Winlock Soaring
P.O. Box 1116

Vancouver 98663
Cascade Wave Flights West
3010 Northeast 44th Street

WEST VIRGINIA
Nitro 25143
Mountaineer Soaring Association
1 Reeves Drive
(Robert Newlon Field)

WISCONSIN
Madison 53715
Madison Soaring, Inc.
1325 North Wingra Drive

Menomonee Falls 53051
Silent Wings, Inc.
Lannon Road
(c/o K. R. Schaarschmidt)

Stoughton 53589
Sky Signs & Aerobatics
832 West Street

Monona 53716
Monona Glider Club
215 Frost Woods Road

Milwaukee 53211
Aerospace Explorer Post 309
2501 Newton
(West Bend Airport)

Osceola 54020
St. Croix Soaring
Box 277

West Bend 53095
West Bend Flying Service
P.O. Box 409

Whitefish Bay 53217
Thermal Sniffers Soaring Club
5007 North Bay Ridge Ave.

WYOMING
Saratoga 82331
Welton Flying Service
P.O. Box 457

Appendix D

Museums

BRADLEY AIR MUSEUM OF THE CONNECTICUT AERONAUTICAL HISTORICAL ASSOCIATION, INC.
Bradley International Airport, Windsor Locks, Connecticut 06096
Telephone: (203) 623-3305

Owned by Connecticut Aeronautical Historical Association. Exhibits of aircraft of various kinds, propulsion systems, and materials associated with aeronautics. Offers a 1,000-volume aeronautics library to researchers (by appointment). Pamphlets, photos, models, and souvenirs for sale. Publishes brochures and a quarterly newsletter.

Open daily 10-6 except for Thanksgiving and Christmas. Admission: $2.50 adults, $1.50 children 5-16 years old, preschool free.

EAA AIR MUSEUM FOUNDATION, INC.
11311 W. Forest Home Avenue (One mile west of Highway 100), Franklin, Wisconsin 53132

Variety of aircraft, including gliders, pre-1900, amateur-built, rotorcraft. Also photos, posters, engines, and propellers. Has a 15,000 volume library of magazines and books on aviation and aeronautics. Presents workshops and forums in its 200-seat auditorium. Publishes a few technical and historical manuals.

Open Monday–Saturday 8:30-5:00; Sunday 11-5. Closed Easter, Thanksgiving, Christmas, New Year's Day. Admission: Adults $2, children $.75.

MUSEUM OF AVIATION GROUP
300 North Spur 341, Fort Worth, Texas 76108
Telephone: (817) 244-1123

Collection of aircraft and associated equipment. Offers a 700-volume aviation library for use on premises.

Open daily 9-5 except Easter and Christmas. No charge.

LYNDON B. JOHNSON SPACE CENTER (NASA)
Office of Public Affairs, Houston, Texas 77058
Telephone: (713) 483-4241

Space shuttle, simulators, anechoic chamber, antenna test range, and other material pertaining to the United States manned space program. Federally operated. Presents lectures in 800-seat auditorium. Cafeteria. Loans exhibitions.

Open daily 9-4, except Christmas. No charge.

NATIONAL AIR AND SPACE MUSEUM
Seventh Street and Independence Avenue, S. W., Washington, D.C. 20560

A bureau of the Smithsonian Institution, a nonprofit, federally chartered corporation. Massive collection of aeronautic and space material, including gliders. Thrilling movies in its large auditorium. Exhibitions occasionally travel. Library of 24,000 volumes available, as well as large collection of photographs.

Open 10-5:30 daily, with extended hours in spring and summer. Closed Christmas. No charge for entrance, but charge for auditorium movies.

NATIONAL SOARING MUSEUM
Harris Hill, RD 1, Elmira, N.Y. 14903

Collection of motorless aircraft; archives of the Soaring Society of America. Houses extensive collection of instruments, photographs, aircraft parts, books, documents, correspondence, and magazines. Maintains the SSA library of soaring films, available for sale or rent. Present building dedicated in 1978.

Open May 16-November 30 daily 11-5. Admission: adults $1.50, students $.50, children free.

PACIFIC MUSEUM OF FLIGHT
PACIFIC NORTHWEST AVIATION HISTORICAL FOUNDATION
400 Broad Street, Seattle, Wa. 98109
Telephone: (206) 692-7106

Variety of sailplanes, powered aircraft, vintage propellers and engines, Boeing 707 fuselage section (used for theater), and scale models. Good library. Gift items for sale. Tours.

Open daily except for New Year's, Easter, Thanksgiving, Christmas. Adults, $1, children $.25.

WRIGHT BROTHERS NATIONAL MEMORIAL
Cape Hattaras National Seashore, Route 1, Box 675, Manteo, NC 27954
Telephone: (919) 473-2111

National Park Service affiliate. Contains replicas of 1902 glider, 1903 flyer, wind tunnel and tools used by the Wrights. Museum located on the site of the Wright Brothers' experiments, next to reconstructed camp buildings. Souvenirs for sale. Tours and lectures.

Open daily 8:30-4:30; summer holidays 8:30-6:30. Closed Christmas. No charge.

Appendix E

Associations

FÉDÉRATION AÉRONAUTIQUE INTERNATIONALE (F.A.I.)
rue Galilee, Paris 16, France

The international organization that gives official recognition of championships, achievements, and records in sporting aviation.

Made up of national aero clubs. The U.S. representative is the National Aeronautic Association (NAA).

Publishes annual report that lists current aviation records, statistical information of various countries, and other data.

Presents such awards as the Lilienthal Medal, accepted as the most distinguished soaring award. Also maintains Registry of Diamond Soaring Badge pilots, sequentially numbered.

ORGANIZATION SCIENTIFIQUE ET TECHNIQUE INTERNATIONAL DU VOL A VOILE (OSTIV)
P.O. Box 9003, The Hague, Netherlands

The international group that has the scientific and technical aspects of soaring as its principal interest.

Founded in 1948 as an associate member of FAI. Membership open to individuals and clubs.

Convenes annually at the World Soaring Championship site to present a forum for the presentation of scientific and technical papers, which subsequently are published in *Technical Soaring* and in the Swiss *Aero Revue*, and collectively as "OSTIV Publications."

Also prints other technical material, such as airworthiness requirements and weight estimations.

Administers various awards and diplomas for noteworthy scientific and technological contributions to soaring, and for significant structural improvement in sailplane design.

THE SOARING SOCIETY OF AMERICA
Suite 25, 3200 Airport Avenue, Santa Monica, CA 90405

Formed in 1932 for the purpose of organizing national soaring competitions. Today recognized as the representative of all gliding interests in the United States. Division of the National Aeronautic Association; designated by the FAI to sanction and conduct contests, adjudge records, award proficiency badges.

Membership: Regular: $28; Student: $18; Life: $450

Publishes the 20,000-circulation *Soaring* and a large number of booklets and lists.

NATIONAL WW II GLIDER PILOTS ASSOCIATION
c/o Connie R. Nanartonis, 23 Woodland Drive, Greenfield, MA 01301

Comprised of about 1,200 of the 6,000 men who flew the Army Air Force's CG-4A combat glider and had a "G" on their silver wings.

Nonprofit; formed 1971; annual reunion.

Publishes quarterly newsletter *Silent Wings*.

THE 1-26 ASSOCIATION

951 Madison, Escondido, CA 92027
Attn: Eddy Gallacher, Secretary-Treasurer

Founded primarily as an owner's organization, now grown to include crew members, families, and other devotees of the Schweizer 1-26. Division of SSA.

Dues: $6 annually for individuals, $1 each for additional family member.

Publishes monthly newsletter, *1-26 Log*

Holds regional and national 1-26 regattas and meets. (The 1-26 is the basis for a one-design class.)
Membership: About 350

THE VINTAGE SAILPLANE ASSOCIATION

3103 Tudor Road, Waldorf, MD 20601
Attn: Pat Storck, Secretary
President: Leonard McClain, West Chester, Pennsylvania
Sponsored by the National Soaring Museum

Membership of more than 200, many of whom are owners of antique sailplanes. Promotes the restoration, flying, and replication of old, classic gliders; collects and maintains through the National Soaring Museum copies of sailplane designs; gathers oral histories.

Membership: $5 annually

Publishes the *Bungee Cord* newsletter

THE EXPERIMENTAL AIRCRAFT ASSOCIATION

P.O. Box 229, Hales Corners, Wisconsin 53130
Paul H. Poberezny, president

A 70,000-member organization interested in home-built aircraft. Publishes periodicals, plans, books. Maintains a 5,000-book library. Holds annual meeting (first week in August) in Oshkosh.

Appendix F

Foreign Sailplane Associations

(Similar in responsibility to SSA)

ALGERIA
Fédération Algérienne des Sports Aeriens,
29 Boulevard Zirout Youcef,
Algiers

ARGENTINA
Fédération Argentine de Vol à Voile,
Anchorena 275,
1170 Buenos Aires

AUSTRALIA
Suite 3, 449 St. Kilda Road,
Melbourne, Victoria 3004

AUSTRIA
Osterreichischer Aero Club,
A—1040 Wien, Prinz-Eugen Strauss 12

BELGIUM
Aéro Club Royal de Belgique,
1, rue Montoyer 1040, Bruxelles

BOLIVIA
Club de Planeadores "Ayar Uchu"
Casilla 1455, La Paz

BRAZIL
Assoc. Brasil. de Voo a Vela,
Caixa Postal 937,
12200 São Jose Dos Campos

BULGARIA
National Aero Club,
48, Boulevard Christo Botev, 1000 Sofia

CANADA
Royal Canadian Flying Clubs,
1815 Alta Vista Drive,
#103 Ottawa, Ontario, K1G 3Y6

CHILI
Federacion Aerea de Chile,
Avenida J. Arrieta N 7698-B,
Casilla Postal 1074

CUBA
Club de Aviacion de Cuba,
Apartado 6215, La Havane

CYPRUS
Cyprus Aero Club,
P.O.B. 4521, Nicosia

CZECHOSLOVAKIA
Aeroklub Ceskoslovenske Social.
Opletalova 29, 11631 Prague 1

DENMARK
kogelig Dansk AeroKlub,
Copenhagen Airport,
Box 68 DKL 4000 Roskilde

EGYPT
Aéro Club d'Egypte
26, rue Cherif, St. Immobilia Building,
Le Caire

ECUADOR
Aero Club del Ecuador,
Avda. de Las Americas,
Casilla 3388, Guayaquil

FINLAND
Finnish Aeronautical Association,
Malmin Airport,
00700 Helsinki 70

FRANCE
Aero Club de France,
6, rue Galilee, 75782 Paris Cedex 16

GERMANY, EAST
Aero Club Republique Democratique,
d'Allemagne 1272 Nuenhagen Berlin

GERMANY, WEST
Deutscsher Aero Club E.V.
6000 Frankfurt-am-Main 71

GREECE
National Aero Club of Greece,
27, Academias Street, Athens

GUERNSEY
The Guernsey Aero Club,
The Airport, La Villiaze-Guernsey

HUNGARY
Fédération Aéronautique de la RPH,
Beloiannisz u. 16, B.P. 382-1054 Budapest

ICELAND
Iceland Aero Club,
Reykjavik Airport, Reykjavik

INDIA
Aero Club India,
United India Life Building,
3rd Floor F Block Connaught Place,
New Delhi 11001

INDONESIA
Aero Club Indonesia,
Tebet Utara Dalam, N 21, Jakarta

IRELAND
Irish Aviation Club,
Dublin Airport, Dublin

ISRAEL
The Aero Club of Israel,
67 Hayarkon Street, P.O.B. 26261,
Tel-Aviv

ITALY
Aero Club d'Italia,
Viale Maresciallo Pilsudski 124, 00197

JAPAN
Japan Aeronautic Assoc.
Koknkaikan Bldg. 1-18-2
Shimbashi Minato-ku Tokyo 105

KOREA, NORTH
Central Aero. Assoc.,
Dongsin 2, Dontaiwon District, Pyongyan

KOREA, SOUTH
Aero. Assoc.,
132-S 1-Ka, Bongnae Dong, Choong-Ku
I.P.O. Box 3855 Seoul

LEBANON
Aero Club du Liban,
P.P. 206, Beyrouth

LIBYA
Aero Club in the Libyan,
Arab Republic, P.O.B. 293, Tripoli

LUXEMBOURG
Aéro Club du Grand Duché de Luxembourg,
Case Postale 2635

MEXICO
Club Aereo Mexico,
Rio de Churubusco—Puerta 9,
Magdalena Mixhuca 8 D.F.

MONACO
Aéro Club de Monaco,
14, Avenue de Fontvieille

MOROCCO
Fédération Ministère de Travaux Publics,
Rabat Chellah

NETHERLANDS
Royal Netherlands Aero. Assoc.,
Josepf Israelsplein 8, The Hague

NEW ZEALAND
Royal New Zealand Aero Club,
P.O. Box 1990, Wellington

NORWAY
Norsk Aero Klubb,
Nedre Slottsgt. 17 Oslo 1

PANAMA
Club Panamericano de Paracaidismo,
Deportivo de Panama: Apartado B Panama 4

PERU
Assoc. Nacional Aero,
Ministerio de Aeron. Fuerza Aerea del Peru
Lima

POLAND
Aeroklub Polskiej,
Krakowskie Przedmiescie 55,
000-071 Warszawa

PORTUGAL
Aero Club de Portugal,
Avenida da Liberdade 226, Lisbonne

RHODESIA
The Central African Soaring Association,
P.O.B. UA 196, Salisbury

ROMANIA
Federation Aeronautique Roumaine,
16, rue Vasile Conta, Bucarest

SOUTH AFRICA
The Aero Club of S. Africa,
109 Winchester House, 25 Loveday Street
Johannesburg, 2001

SPAIN
Real Aero Club de España,
Carrera de San Jeronimo 15, Madrid 14

SWEDEN
Royal Swedish Aero Club,
Skeppsbron 40 Box 1212,
S 11182 Stockholm

SWITZERLAND
Aero Club de Suisse,
Lidostrasse 5, CH 6006, Lucerne

TUNISIA
Fédération Tunisienne des Sports Aériens,
17, avenue Habib Bourguiba, Tunis

TURKEY
Turkish Air League,
Ataturk Bulvari, 33, Ankara

U.S.S.R.
Federatsia Aviatsionnogo Sporta SSSR,
B.P. 395 Moscow 123362

UNITED KINGDOM
Royal Aero Club,
Kimberley House, Vaughan Way,
Leicester LE1 4SG

VENEZUELA
Aero Club Caracas,
Apartado 2057, Caracas

YUGOSLAVIA
Aeronautical Union,
Uzun Mirkova 4/1 E.P. 872 11000 Belgrade

ZAMBIA
National Aero Club of Zambia,
P.O.B. 1016, Mufulira

Appendix G

Conversion Tables

RATE OF CLIMB
CONVERSION SCALE

KNOTS	METRES PER SEC	FT/MIN	FT/SEC	KM/H	MPH
1		100	1	1	1
			2	2	
2	1	200	3	3	2
			4	4	
3		300	5	5	3
4	2	400	6	6	4
			7	7	
				8	5
5		500	8	9	
			9	10	6
6	3	600	10	11	7
			11	12	
7		700	12	13	8
8	4	800	13	14	9
			14	15	
9		900	15	16	10
			16	17	11
10	5	1000	17	18	
				19	12
11		1100	18	20	
12	6	1200	19	21	13
			20	22	14
			21	23	
13		1300	22	24	15
14	7	1400	23	25	
			24	26	16
15		1500	25	27	17
			26	28	
16	8	1600	27	29	18
				30	
17		1700	28	31	19
	9		29	32	20
18		1800	30	33	
			31	34	21
19	10	1000	32	35	22
		2000	33	36	

SPEED CONVERSION SCALE

KNOTS	MPH	KM/H	FT/SEC
10	10	10	10
		20	20
20	20	30	30
	30	40	40
30		50	50
	40	60	60
40		70	70
	50	80	80
50		90	90
	60	100	
60	70	110	100
		120	110
70	80	130	120
		140	130
80	90	150	140
	100	160	150
90		170	160
	110	180	170
100		190	
	120	200	180
110		210	190
	130	220	200
120	140	230	210
130	150	240	220
		250	230
140	160	260	240
		270	
150	170		250

CONVERSION FACTORS

To Convert	Into Distance	Multiply by
Centimeters	Inches	0.3973
Feet	Meters	0.3048
Feet	Kilometers	3048
Feet	Nautical miles	6076
Feet, square	Square meters	0.0929
Inches	Centimeters	2.540
Inches, square	Square centimeters	6.451
Kilometers	Meters	1000
Kilometers	Nautical miles	0.5396
Kilometers	Statute miles	0.6214
Meters	Feet	3.2808
Meters	Kilometers	1000
Meters	Nautical miles	539.6
Meters	Yards	1.0936
Miles, nautical	Feet	6080
Miles, nautical	Kilometer	1.852
Miles, nautical	Statute miles	1.1515
Miles, statute	Feet	5280
Miles, statute	Kilometers	1.609
Miles, statute	Nautical miles	0.8684

To Convert	Into Weight	Multiply by
Grams	Ounces	0.035
Kilograms	Ounces	35.27
Kilograms	Pounds	2.205
Ounces	Grams	28.35
Pounds	Kilograms	0.4536

To Convert	Into Volume	Multiply by
Gallons	Liters	3.78
Liters	Gallons	0.264
Liters	Ounces	33.81
Liters	Pints	2.10
Liters	Quarts	1.05
Liters	Cubic inches	61.02
Pints	Liters	0.47
Quarts	Liters	0.95

To Convert	Into Temperature	Multiply by
Fahrenheit	Centigrade	5/9 (F–32)
Centigrade	Fahrenheit	(9/5C) + 32

To Convert	Into Water Volume/Weight	Multiply by
Liters	Pounds	2.2
Cubic feet	Pounds	62.4
Gallon, imperial	Pounds	10.0
Gallon, U.S.	Liters	3.78
Gallons, U.S.	Pounds	8.35
Gallons, U.S.	Cubic meter	.0037
Liters	U.S. gallons	0.264
Pounds	Gallons, U.S.	0.12
Pounds	Milliliters	453.56

To Convert	Into Pressure	Multiply by
Kg/sq cm	Lb/sq inch	14.3
Kg/sq meter	Lb/sq foot	0.205
Pounds/sq inch	Kg/sq cm	0.07
Pounds/sq foot	Kg/sq meter	4.882

To Convert   Into Map Scales

1/250,000 = .257 inch to the statute mile (approximately 1/4 inch to the mile)
= 0.292 inch to the nautical mile
1/500,000 = 0.127 inch to the statute mile (approximately 1/8 inch to the mile)
= 0.146 inch to the nautical mile

	knots	mph	km/hr	m/sec	100 ft/min	ft/sec
knot	1	1.1515	1.8532	0.5148	1.014	1.6889
1 mph	0.8684	1	1.609	0.447	0.88	1.4667
1 km/hr	0.5396	0.6214	1	0.2778	0.5468	0.9113
1 m/sec	1.9424	2.2369	3.6	1	1.968	3.2808
100 f/min	0.9868	1.136	1.829	0.508	1	1.667
1 ft/sec	0.5921	0.6818	1.0973	0.3048	0.6	1

Appendix H

Abbreviations and Acronyms

AGL — Above-ground level

ASI — Airspeed indicator

ASL — Above sea level

ATC — Air traffic control

CAS — Calibrated airspeed

CB SIT CB — Acronym to remember pretakeoff cockpit check: Controls, ballast, straps, instruments, trim, canopy, brakes

CFI — Certified flight instructor

Cu — Cumulus cloud

CuNum — Cumulonimbus cloud

EAS — Equivalent airspeed

FAA — Federal Aviation Administration

FAI — Fédération Aéronautique Internationale

FAR — Federal Aviation Regulation

FCC — Federal Communications Commission

FSS — Flight Service Station

G — Gravity

IAS — Indicated airspeed

IFR — Instrument flight rules

L/D — Lift over drag (glide ratio)

MCA — Minimum controllable airspeed

MOA — Military operation area

MSL — Mean sea level

NDB — Nondirectional radio beacon

OAR — Acronym to remember three documents required to be in glider cockpit: Operations limitations (or Owner's manual), Airworthiness certificate, and Registration

O&R — Out and return

OSTIV — Organisation Scientifique et Technique International du Vol à Voile

PIO — Pilot-induced oscillations

SSA — Soaring Society of America

TAS — True airspeed

TCA — Terminal Control Area

TLAR — "That Looks About Right" (see Glossary)

Vα — Maneuvering speed

Vb — Design speed for maximum gust intensity

Vd — Diving speed

Vf — Design flap speed

Vfe — Maximum flap extended speed

VFR — Visual flight rules

VHF — Very high frequency

Vle — Maximum landing gear extended speed

Vlo — Maximum landing gear operating speed

Vne — Never-exceed speed

VOR — Very high frequency OmniRange station

Vs — Stalling speed or minimum speed at which plane is controllable

Vso — Stalling speed or minimum steady flight speed in the landing configuration

Appendix I

Private Pilot (Glider Rating) Test Guide

(Adapted and condensed from Part 61 of the Federal Aviation Regulations (FAR). For *specific* information, review the applicable sections of the regulations.)

To be eligible for a Private Certificate with a glider rating, an applicant must pass a written exam and a flight test, unless he is a licensed power-plane pilot, in which case a written test is not required.

Written Tests

The written tests are comprehensive, because to be effective they must test an applicant's knowledge in many areas. They may contain as many as 50 test items. Three-and-a-half hours are allowed for taking each test.

All test questions are the objective, multiple-choice type, and each is independent of every other test item—that is, a correct response to one test item does not depend upon the correct response to another item.

After completing the test, the applicant's answer sheet is forwarded to the FAA Aeronautical Center for scoring. The applicant then receives an Airman Written Test Report, which not only includes the score, but lists the subject areas in which difficulty is experienced.

Taking the Tests

The FAA takes considerable effort to write each test item unambiguously, and so applicants should read carefully the information and instructions, as well as each test item. Points to remember when taking the test:

1. There are no "trick" questions. Don't look for hidden meanings.

2. Carefully read the entire test item, statement, or question before looking at the answers below it. Skimming and hasty assumptions can lead to an erroneous approach to a problem.

3. Only one of the answers given is completely correct. The alternatives may be the result of using incorrect procedures to solve problems, common misconceptions, or incomplete knowledge of the subject. If the subject matter is understood, answering the questions should not be difficult.

4. If considerable difficulty is experienced with a particular test item, the applicant should not spend too much time on it, but continue on with other items that are less difficult. When easier items are completed, go back and complete the difficult questions.

The Applicant's Library

To enhance professionalism in the field of aviation, the prospective pilot should establish and maintain a technical library, and he begins by obtaining study materials that help him to prepare for certification. The following list presents essential reference material, but does not, of course, include all the useful publications available.

Airman's Information Manual. (From GPO.) Presents, in five parts, information necessary for planning and conducting flights within the National Airspace System. Each part is available on a separate annual subscription.

The American Soaring Handbook. Published by the Soaring Society of America, this handbook represents the combined efforts of many veteran soaring pilots. Each chapter is a separate booklet. Write SSA (Box 66071, Los Angeles, California 90066) for current prices.

Aviation Weather, AC 00-6A. (From GPO.) Contains information on weather for those whose interest is primarily in its application to flying. It includes material on aviation weather services, glossary of meteorological terms, a chapter devoted to soaring weather, and many illustrations.

Aviation Weather Services, AC 00-45. (From GPO.) A supplement to AC 00-6A, periodically updated to reflect changes. It explains current weather services and the uses of weather charts and printed weather messages in detail, and is an excellent source of study for pilot-certification examinations.

Federal Aviation Regulations. Suggested parts for study: Part 1, Definitions and Abbreviations. Part 61, Certification: Pilots and Flight Instructors. Part 91, General Operating and Flight Rules. Available from the Government Printing Office (GPO).

National Transportation Safety Board Procedural Regulation, Part 830. Deals with required notification and reporting procedures relating to aircraft accidents and lost or overdue aircraft. It is free from the National Transportation Safety Board, Publications Section, Washington, D.C. 20594.

Pilot's Handbook of Aeronautical Knowledge, AC 61-23A. Contains authoritative information used in training private and commercial pilots. It is designed primarily for the airplane pilot, but much of the material is applicable to glider pilot students.

Wake Turbulence, AC 90-23A. Presents information and suggests techniques that may help pilots avoid the hazards associated with wingtip vortex turbulence. Free from the Department of Transportation, Distribution Unit, TAD 443.1, Washington, D.C. 20590.

Author's note: Here are three other books you might want to add to your basic library:

Glider Basics, by Thomas Knauff. Available from the author at Ridge Soaring, Inc., Julian, Pennsylvania 16844.

Soaring Flight Manual, published by Jeppesen Sanderson, Inc., under the guidance of the SSA.

Understanding Gliding, by Derek Piggott (A & C Black Limited, 35 Bedford Row, London Wc1R4JH).

Sample Test Questions

The following test items are given to familiarize applicants with the *type* of questions that may be found on the written tests. Keep in mind that they contain only a few of the topics found on the actual test.

1. Rules and procedures pertaining to the notification and reporting of aircraft accidents can be found in:
   1 - Federal Aviation Regulations, Part 61.
   2 - Federal Aviation Regulations, Part 91.
   3 - Federal Aviation Regulations, Part 63.
   4 - National Transportation Safety Board, Part 830.

Answer 4 is correct.

2. Aircraft documents that are required by Federal Aviation Regulations to be on board a civil aircraft during flight are the:

1 - logbook and Registration Certificate.
2 - owner's handbook and Registration Certificate.
3 - logbook and Airworthiness Certificate.
4 - Registration and Airworthiness Certificates.

Answer 4 is correct.

3. An aircraft towing a glider has the right-of-way over all:

1 - other aircraft.
2 - other engine-driven aircraft.
3 - airships and balloons.
4 - gliders in free flight.

Answer 2 is correct.

4. If the field elevation at an airport in controlled airspace is 1,900 feet, and the sky conditions at this airport is reported as 20 SCT M50 OVC, the highest altitude at which a glider could be operated beneath the ceiling to remain in VFR conditions would be approximately:

1 - 6,400 feet MSL.
2 - 3,400 feet MSL.
3 - 4,500 feet MSL.
4 - 1,500 feet MSL.

Answer 1 is correct.

5. The intensity of vortices associated with the wake turbulence created by large airplanes is greatest when such airplanes are operating at:

1 - low airspeeds and high gross weights.
2 - high airspeeds and high gross weights.
3 - high airspeeds and low gross weights.
4 - low airspeeds and low gross weights.

Answer 1 is correct.

Questions (but no answers) intended to direct study to selected areas in which there are likely to be questions.

1. How often is an inspection required for a sailplane used for hire?
2. What certificates are required to be in the possession of a pilot when flying solo in a sailplane?
3. What are the right-of-way rules that apply to glider operation?
4. What "recent experience" is required to act as pilot in command of a glider for solo flight? For carrying passengers?
5. Describe the general safety rules that apply to the use of oxygen.
6. According to regulations, what are the differences in preparing for a cross-country flight as opposed to a flight in the vicinity of the departure airport?
7. Differentiate between an airport traffic area and a control zone.
8. What information that would be useful to a sailplane pilot can be found in the Airman's Information Manual, Part II?
9. What are the magnetic compass errors, and how are they compensated?
10. As used in navigation, what is the difference between a true course and a magnetic course?

11. If a sailplane covered a distance of 62 nautical miles in 1 hour and 23 minutes, what was the average groundspeed?

12. Draw a profile of a proposed cross-country flight for a sailplane, including altitudes at "go ahead" points considering winds.

13. What is the basic purpose of applying weather reports and forecasts to a proposed flight and analyzing the weather as the flight progresses?

14. If atmospheric instability exists, what weather conditions can be expected?

15. What effect does a change in air density have on the operation of a sailplane?

16. List the requirements for the occurrence of standing waves with appreciable vertical currents.

17. What effect does the ridge shape have on the strength of any lift produced by it?

18. What is the effect of wind and wind shear on thermals?

19. The maximum strength of both the thermals and the downdrafts depends mainly upon what atmospheric phenomena?

20. How is lift generated by a wing?

21. If a rope break occurred at an altitude of 200 feet above ground level, what would you do?

22. What is the recommended procedure if it becomes necessary to land the sailplane while being towed by the towplane?

23. What is the recommended procedure to use during landing on a hill?

24. Explain the meaning of glide ratio or L/D. What effect does airspeed and wind have on glide ratio?

25. If too low on final approach, what is the recommended procedure? If too high on final approach?

26. At what altitude is supplemental oxygen required?

27. How is the maximum speed for an auto or a winch tow determined?

28. What is the recommended procedure to use during an auto or a winch tow if the cable cannot be released from the sailplane?

29. What is the recommended normal procedure for releasing from a winch tow? An airplane tow?

30. During a winch tow, how is the airspeed of the sailplane increased or decreased?

Glossary

Adverse yaw See Aileron drag.

Aileron Movable panel at the trailing edge of each wing near the tip, used to control bank or rolling movements.

Aileron drag (adverse yaw) Shift in the nose of the plane sideways against the direction of desired turn caused by ailerons. Compensation is with the rudder. (See Yaw.)

Airfoil Wing, tail or other surface shaped to deflect the air through which it moves to produce a desired reaction.

Airplane An engine-driven fixed-wing aircraft that is supported in flight by the dynamic reaction of the air against its wings. (FAA definition.)

Airspeed The speed of an aircraft in relation to the air. *Indicated* airspeed is the reading of the airspeed indicator. *True* airspeed is the indicated airspeed corrected for air density.

Airworthiness certificate A verification of the most recent annual inspection, displayed in the sailplane.

Altimeter Instrument indicating either height above the landing field or above mean sea level, depending on how it was set before takeoff.

Anabatic wind Air rising adjacent to sun-warmed slope.

Angle of attack The angle between the wing's mean chord line and the direction of the relative wind. (Not to be confused with pitch.)

Angle of incidence The angle between the wing chord and the sailplane's longitudinal axis. Angle is not adjustable by pilot, but fixed by manufacturer when wing is attached to fuselage.

Aspect ratio The ratio between the span (from tip to tip) and the mean chord (width) of the wings.

Attitude Position, stance, or aspect of the sailplane as determined by the inclination about any of its three axes.

Auto tow Method of launching glider by towing it with a motor vehicle.

Axis The line extending through the center of gravity in each major plane: longitudinal, lateral, vertical.

Bank To roll about the longitudinal axis.

Barogram The flight recording or "track" made by a barograph.

Barograph A recording aneroid barometer used by sailplane pilots to show altitude and time during flight.

Benign spiral The maneuver some sailplanes assume if, properly trimmed, the pilot removes hands and feet from controls; sometimes used to descend through clouds.

Best glide speed The indicated airspeed that produces the flattest glide possible in still air.

Bernoulli effect A fluid in motion exerts decreasing pressure as its speed increases.

Biplane Aircraft with double wing.

Buffeting The shudder before a stall caused by the turbulent wake of the wing.

Camber The cross-sectional curvature of the wing.

Center of gravity Point of balance; if supported by this center with three degrees of freedom, the sailplane would balance in any position.

Chart Aeronautical map.

Checkpoint Easily identifiable spot on the chart or ground, used to navigate.

Chord line A straight line from the leading to the trailing edge of a wing or other airfoil; often simply "chord."

Clean Said of a sailplane that has little parasitic drag; also said of smooth, coordinated flying.

Clear Condition in which nearby areas are empty of other personnel or aircraft.

Cloud base Altitude of flat bottom of cumulus clouds.

Cloud street Row of cumulus clouds organized by windflow.

Control surface The ailerons, elevator, rudder, flaps, dive brakes, etc.

Convection The vertical movement of a column of air because of temperature differential; the driving force of thermals.

Convergence The confluence of two moving bodies of air, often producing lift.

Coordination Simultaneous use of the aileron and rudder in such a way that the yaw string and the slip-skid ball remain centered.

Crabbing Simultaneous forward and sideways flight, usually to counteract for wind drift; also called wind-correction angle.

Critical angle of attack The point at which the angle of attack has become so great that the wing stalls.

Cross-control stall See Incipient spin.

Crossed controls Simultaneous application of opposite rudder and aileron.

Cumulonimbus (CuNum) Cloud associated with thunderstorm; cumulus cloud that has begun to produce rain.

Cumulus (Cu) Cloud associated with thermal activity.

Decay Said of a disintegrating cloud as its lift disappears.

Deviation The compass error caused by metal or electrical forces in the sailplane.

Diamond Soaring award earned for distance beyond 310.7 miles (500 km), a flight of at least 186.4 miles (300 km) to a predetermined goal, or an altitude gain of at least 16,404 feet (5,000 m).

Diamond mine Good location to earn diamonds.

Dihedral Inclination of wing upward from roots to tips.

Dive Steep forward descent.

Dive brakes Vertical plates that the pilot extends above and/or below wings to create drag and reduce lift.

Downwash The air pushed downward by a wing.

Drag The force exerted opposite to the direction of flight.

Drift The angle between a plane's path and its heading, caused by wind; angle between course and direction in which nose is pointing.

Drogue chute Deployable parachute attached to the tail to permit shorter landings.

Dual controls Two complete sets of controls so that either party in craft can fly.

Elevator Hinged horizontal surface at the tail used to control the angle of attack, and thus the speed.

Empennage The whole tail, including both fixed and movable elements.

Fairing Rigid material on sailplane surface to smooth the airflow and to reduce drag.

Federal Aviation Administration (FAA) The central governmental regulating body of civil aviation in the United States.

Fédération Aéronautique Internationale (FAI) The worldwide governing body of aeronautical contests and keeper of world records.

Fin (vertical stabilizer) Fixed vertical tail surface to which rudder is hinged, used to provide yaw stability.

Flaps Hinged panels of the trailing edge of wings between the ailerons and fuselage, to increase airfoil shape, thereby increasing lift and drag.

Flare (flare-out; roundout) In landing, the change in flight path from descending to one parallel with the surface, just before touchdown.

Foehn wind A dry, warm wind blowing down a mountain slope, known by dozens of local names around the world; e.g., chinook, of the Rockies.

Foehn gap Blue strip of sky surrounded by wave cloud; more specifically, area between mountain's lap cloud and its first lenticular cloud.

Fuselage The body of an aircraft.

G The measuring unit of load on a sailplane's structure stated in terms of multiples of the force of gravity.

Gaggle A group of sailplanes in a thermal.

Glass ship Sailplane made of fiberglass.

Glide Coasting downhill on the air.

Glider Winged aircraft using no power source other than gravity. All sailplanes are gliders, but some gliders are designed only for descent, not for soaring.

Glide ratio Ratio of movement forward to downward; same as the ratio of lift to drag; L/D; one measure of a glider's performance.

Glide slope Descending path of glider; same as glide ratio in still air under standard atmospheric conditions.

Ground effect The increase in support of air close to the ground caused by its compression between the wings and the ground.

Ground loop A violent, uncontrolled turn on the ground, usually upon landing, usually caused by wing touching the ground or foliage.

Ground speed Speed relative to the earth, regardless of wind.

Hang glider A lightweight glider (usually less than 100 pounds) from which the pilot is suspended.

Heading An aircraft's course corrected for wind drift; may be compass, true, or magnetic. Direction sailplane is pointed in regardless of flight path.

Heat of condensation Heat generated and released into the surrounded air (providing increased upward movement) when a thermal changes to visible cloud.

High-speed stall Stall occurring at any speed above normal, level-flight stall speed; does not involve high-speed flight.

High tow The aerotow position above the towplane's wake.

Incipient spin The single-wing stall that is considered to be the first step toward a spin.

Inclinometer See Slip-skid ball.

Induced drag The rearward-acting component of lift, decreasing with airspeed.

Inversion layer Point at which air no longer is growing colder with altitude.

Isogonic line A line connecting points of equal magnetic variation on maps, used when computing magnetic course.

Katabatic wind Air sliding down a shaded slope.

Knot One international nautical mile or international air mile (6,080.1 feet, or 1,852 meters) per hour.

Landing speed Indicated airspeed at touchdown.

Lapse rate Rate of temperature and pressure change with altitude.

Launch Method of starting glider on flight, usually aerotow, auto launch or winch launch.

L/D Lift divided by drag; numerically the same as the glide ratio, or the ratio of forward to downward motion (spoken "L over D").

L/D speed Airspeed at which plane achieves its maximum glide ratio. (For comparison see Sink.)

Leading edge Forward edge of an airfoil; opposite the trailing edge.

Lee wave See Wave.

Lenticular cloud Lens-shaped cloud of a mountain wave.

Lift Upward-moving air currents strong enough to carry a sailplane up. Also the upward force of an airfoil as it moves through the air.

Load The forces acting on the sailplane. *Static* load is the weight. *Gross* load is the maximum weight, including pilot, passenger and luggage. *Useful* load is the difference between the empty load and the maximum authorized weight. *Maneuvering* loads are those induced by the controls. *Gust* loads are those caused by air currents.

Load factor Total of the maneuvering loads expressed in Gs. The *limit* load factor is the figure beyond which structural damage may occur.

Log Collected records of each flight.

Loop Vertical aerobatic circle maneuver.

Low tow In aerotow, the position of the glider below the towplane's wake.

MacCready speed ring Scale surrounding variometer that is turned to show speed to fly between thermals for best overall ground speed.

Maneuvering speed The speed above which the load factor may cause structural damage by abrupt maneuvers.

Maximum L/D airspeed Airspeed at which a glider achieves its best glide ratio.

Minimum controllable airspeed See Slow flight.

Minimum sink rate Speed in feet per second in which a glider descends at optimal airspeed in calm weather.

Minimum sink speed Airspeed at which the glider loses altitude most slowly—a few mph above stall speed, and somewhat below best glide speed. Figure helps to describe glider's efficiency. (For comparison, see L/D speed.)

Motorglider Sailplane with engine designed to be turned off in lift.

Mountain wave See wave.

N Letter designating United States, appearing as first character of FAA aircraft registration, and on SSA pins and FAI badges.

National Aeronautic Association (NAA) The U.S. body delegated by the FAI to process records in the U.S. and to govern contests. For soaring, this work is done by SSA, an NAA division.

Netto Device that subtracts aircraft sink rate, regardless of airspeed, from the variometer reading, leaving a reading that shows the sink rate of the airmass that the glider is in.

Open-class gliders In competition, the class that allows any glider to enter, regardless of wingspan, etc.; indicates high performance.

Out and return Flight to predetermined site and back.

Overbanking tendency In a steep turn, the outer wing travels faster than the inner wing, thus developing more lift and tending to steepen the angle of bank.

Overdevelopment A condition in which so many cumulus clouds accumulate that the sun is largely blocked from warming the ground, and the thermal lift slows or stops.

Overshoot To land beyond the intended spot; opposite: undershoot.

Parasitic drag Resistance of sailplane to passage through the air, varying directly with speed.

Penetrate To achieve a groundspeed despite strong headwind.

Pilotage Navigation by watching for landmarks.

Pitch Attitude of the nose, high or low; angle of the longitudinal axis to the horizon. (Not to be confused with angle of attack.)

Pitot tube Tube, open end facing forward in front of the glider, to measure impact air pressure, the source of pressure for air-operated instruments. Pronounced "pee*tow*."

Placard A statement of operation limitations required to be affixed where it can be seen by the pilot during flight.

Polar curve A sailplane's performance plotted by speed and sink rate.

Porpoising Traveling with wavelike pitches, like a porpoise.

Redline A red warning mark on airspeed indicator to identify maximum speed without endangering the aircraft; coincides with the maximum appearing on the placard. Also called "never-exceed speed."

Registration certificate Statement of ownership and listing of identity numbers. It must be displayed to be seen when sailplane is on the ground.

Relative airflow (relative wind) Apparent movement of air in respect to body travelling through it.

Release Device for dropping tow rope from plane; also, the act of disengaging rope.

Retrieve Trip to disassemble and bring back a glider by car and trailer, or an aerotow from off-field landing.

Ridge soaring Using wind moving up a slope to maintain lift.

Rollout Path of a landing sailplane from touchdown to stop.

Rotor The swirling, turbulent circulation under the top of a mountain wave, often indicated by ragged, wispy clouds.

Roundover or roundout In a ground launch, the period near release when the rate of climb drops and the glider nears a normal gliding attitude.

Rudder The hinged, vertical surface attached to the vertical stabilizer used to counteract aileron drag.

Sailplane Used to indicate higher-performance glider, and to distinguish from military gliders; a glider designed for soaring.

Sea-breeze front Confluence of cool wind moving in from ocean and warm land air.

Separation (burble) Turbulence on the top of an airfoil.

Shear line Point at which air masses moving at different directions or speeds meet.

Sink Descending air in which the glider loses altitude faster than in still air; when applied to a sailplane, rate at which it loses altitude in still air, commonly expressed in feet per second. (See Minimum sink.)

Skid Sideways motion relative to the air with wings level, or, in a turn, the tendency to slide toward the upper wing; also, skilike runner under fuselage forward from or in place of the front wheel.

Slip Sideways slide of a glider toward the lowered wing.

Slip-skid ball (inclinometer) A ball immersed in fluid rolling in a U-shaped glass tube indicating whether the aircraft is slipping, skidding, or stable.

Slow flight (minimum controllable airspeed) Flight at a speed just above the indications of stall, where any additional load or reduction in speed would produce stall warnings.

Soar To fly without an engine and without losing altitude.

Soaring Society of America (SSA) Organization delegated by the National Aeronautic Association to govern soaring contests and to monitor record flights in the United States, and to represent soaring interests before the regulatory agencies of government.

Sock (windsock) Cloth cone, open at ends and hung from a pole, to indicate wind direction. Large end points upwind.

Span Distance from wing tip to wing tip.

Speed-to-fly The optimum speed that a pilot should fly, taking into consideration the surrounding mass of air; the optimum speed to maintain between thermals to maximize cross-country speed.

Spin Nose-down, corkscrewlike, near-vertical descent, with at least one wing stalled, yaw string to side, speed stable.

Spiral dive High-speed, nearly uncontrolled, downward series of turns, with wings unstalled, at a continually accelerating speed.

Spoilers Small panels or slats in some sailplanes that the pilot raises vertically to disturb the airflow across the wing top, decreasing *(spoiling)* lift and increasing drag to accelerate descent.

Stability The tendency to maintain and to return to straight and level flight without pilot help if the attitude is disturbed.

Stabilizer The fixed horizontal and vertical tail surfaces used to dampen pitch and yaw.

Stable air Mass of air that tends to remain stratified, resisting thermal development.

Stall Condition resulting when air no longer produces lift sufficient to hold an aircraft's altitude.

Stalling speed The airspeed at which the wing stalls.

Standard-class sailplane One that conforms to 15-meter span restriction, as established by OSTIV and adopted by FAI.

Static source Opening or port on the aircraft that is at neutral pressure at all speeds and normal flight attitudes; used for instruments.

Stick Control rod grasped by the pilot that moves the ailerons and elevator.

Stick thermal Upward swing of variometer indicator (or audio indication of lift) caused by abrupt back pressure on control stick, sometimes interpreted as rising air.

Terminal velocity The highest speed attainable in a dive or free fall. Can be controlled with drag-producing devices.

Thermal A heated, rising column, bubble, or cone of air from the earth's surface that is penetrating surrounding cooler air.

Thermaling Climbing in a thermal.

TLAR "That Looks About Right," a landing sequence based on the pilot's ability to judge approach angles.

Total energy variometer An altitude-change indicator designed to ignore variations in airspeed (and often interpreted as altitude change) caused by turbulence or abrupt stick movements.

Towline Usually 1/4-inch, plastic rope about 150 feet long with a steel ring at each end, one for the glider, one for the towplane.

Track Ground path over which the aircraft flies.

Trim control Lever or wheel that adjusts elevator tabs or a spring that exerts mild force on the elevator-control system, to reduce the need for constant stick pressure.

Unstable air An air mass in which verticle movements of air (commonly thermals) move easily.

Variation The angle comprising the difference between true and magnetic north.

Variometer A sensitive and quick rate-of-climb/rate-of-descent instrument, used to show slight changes in altitude; the basic soaring instrument.

Venturi tube Tube with a narrow section designed to produce a suction by the Bernoulli effect.

Wake The turbulent, mostly downward-moving air behind an aircraft.

Wave Undulating wind current in lee of mountain.

Weak link Section of rope spliced into a towline specified by the FAA to be of a certain maximum strength, as a safety measure.

Wind shadow Area of calm downwind of hills, buildings, rows of trees, and other windbreaks.

Wind shear Shift in wind direction or velocity with altitude.

Wind shift Sharp change in the surface wind that can complicate landings.

Wind velocity gradient Change of wind speed with height above ground, usually increasing with altitude.

Wing loading Gross weight of an aircraft divided by its wing area, to indicate one measure of efficiency.

Yaw Rotation around a vertical axis (to turn flatly from side to side).

Yaw string A 3-inch (or so) piece of yarn tied or taped before the pilot on the center line of the canopy or on the pitot tube; indicates a slip or skid by blowing to the side.

Zero sink Condition in which upward movement or air equals glider's minimum descent rate, so that the aircraft's altitude remains constant.

Index